Put That Knife Away

Phyllis W Palm

Alzheimer's, Marriage and My Transformation from Wife to Caregiver

Phyllis W. Palm, PhD

Dedication

For Steve, who cares so much, for Linda and Dave, Ted, Austin and Grant who travel with me on this journey of love

and

For the family caregivers, unsung, unpaid, who unselfishly devote a great part of their lives to caring for someone they love who is no longer able to be responsible for him or herself.

Table of Contents

1 – A Rude Awakening   1

2 – Initial Symptoms of
Memory Loss   6

3 – First Neurology Consults   17

4 – So What IS Normal Aging?   34

5 – Personality Changes   41

6 – I Need Help   51

7 – Sexual Misbehavior   53

8 – Good Adjustments   59

9 – Finding Meaningful Work   67

10 – And Still More Diagnoses   72

11 – A Good Combination   82

12 – Freedom from Want   89

13 – Tangles and Plaques   100

14 – Children Visit   105

15 – Time Changes   112

16 – Tenacity   120

17 – Insight   125

18 – Hired Helpers Saga   134

19 – What is Selfish?   145

20 – Psychotic Break in Arizona   150

21 – Avon-by-the-Sea   156

22 – Social Misbehaviors   160

23 – Happy Birthday   164

24 – Emotional Bank Account   168

25 – Just like in Morocco   173

26 – The Pile-Up   179

27 – Family Thanksgiving   181

28 – Worries   186

29 – Memory Loss Awareness   191

30 – Leon's Story   196

31 – Scary New Behavior   204

32 – Alex's Story   208

33 – Overly Significant
        Everyday Experiences   215

34 – Out in Limbo-Dismissed by the
        Movement Disorders Clinic   218

35 – Metaphor for My Life Today   221

36 – Was This a Constructive Day?   228

37 – Delusions and Hallucinations   231

38 – Put That Knife Away   235

39 – The Psychiatric Hospital   248

40 – Agida   254

41 – Seven to Ten Days   257

42 – The Decision   263

43 – A New Era   265

44 – Initial Visits   275

45 – Insight Redux   280

Acknowledgements

I am profoundly grateful to Mindy Lewis and my classmates, Sandra Ceslowitz, Susan Charney, Betsy Spiegel, Connie Sommer, Megan Jeanne, Joan Tedeschi, Anna Grundstrom, Nancy Stiefel and Pamela Theodoredis at The Writer's Voice of the West Side YMCA for teaching me, supporting me, reading and critiquing many beginning chapters as I learned to find my voice. I am thankful to Claire Berman and to Mindy Lewis for their expertise in editing my first manuscript, and I am forever indebted to my dear friend and fellow psychologist, Dr. Amy Schaffer, who painstakingly edited each chapter more than once to help clear up any professional issues.

I am so appreciative of my dear cousin Eleonora Wenner who has devoted enormous amounts of time, skill and energy to all the many stages of my manuscript, copyediting, proofreading, formatting and publishing. Nora lives in Zurich, Switzerland and we communicate via Skype and email, building our relationship as we work on this project together.

I thank all of the caregivers who willingly permitted me to listen to and use their stories for inclusion in this book. I thank all of the people, social workers and caregivers who participate with me in support groups and whose experience and advice I cherish. It is my fervent hope that our stories will be of help to other family caregivers tasked with the impossible situation of caring for a loved one whose mood and skills decrease without regularity, whose needs change every ten minutes; and who while functioning to the best of their ability and with the last of their strength are constantly bombarded by well-intentioned advice from relatives, friends or physicians who phone or visit or examine our loved ones several times a year.

1 – A Rude Awakening

New York, January 2008

"You have got to stop her. She only wants my money. She can't wait for me to die. She's cheating my children out of their inheritance," my husband of eighteen years is screaming uncontrollably. He says much more as I walk into the room where Bob is speaking with our attorney. We arrive at her office on a Sunday morning in January 2008 to ask Mrs. G. to review a contract of sale on a winter home we are purchasing in Arizona. Bob starts screaming at me, "Get out of here. I want to talk to the lawyer myself." The lawyer nods, indicating that she is all right and I back out of the room. *I can't believe what's happening. I feel lost in a nightmare. Maybe I'll wake up and realize this is my anxiety about buying a house.*

Mrs. G. has our important papers file. She knows we have carefully planned our estate. We have wills, powers of attorney and medical proxies in place since 1990 when we married. We updated these documents in 2005, when we moved from New Jersey to New York. I sit in the next office and listen as she takes our paperwork from her safe and explains to Bob the fair way we have set up money from his savings, mine and ours. He doesn't remember doing this work, but he sees the dates and his signature and he trusts her. When he is calm, she asks him to sit in the waiting room for a few minutes and calls me in.

"Phyllis," she says somberly, "I don't think you should buy this house. Your husband, in my opinion, is too upset to sign a contract."

Yikes, this is no dream. It is real. Mrs. G. is worried. I can see it.

"This is the first inkling I have that any of this has been brewing inside Bob," I tell her. "He's the one who wanted this house. He fell in love with the backyard fruit trees and the garage workshop. I'm not the one pushing this."

She reaches out, puts her hand on my arm to calm me and explains slowly that there is a clause in the contract which will allow for the return of our deposit and let us out of the sale. We walk out to the waiting room together after this decision is reached. Bob looks up from the magazine he's reading, says he's hungry and asks the attorney for a restaurant recommendation in her office neighborhood. She joins us for lunch. *If I told anyone in the restaurant what has just transpired, they would think I was off my rocker.* Bob is calm, friendly and talkative as he orders from the menu. Everything looks normal.

Once we get home, Bob is agitated and abusive once more. On Monday, as I'm about to leave for my office, he becomes insulting and nasty. "You whore. You nasty bitch. Where are you going? You must be meeting other men. You must be; you won't have sex with me. You jump out of bed early in the morning and you roll over at night. We used to have sex all the time. I don't know what happened to you." *I can't believe this is my husband talking. He hates cursing. I am the one who uses foul language occasionally. He never has. Until now.*

His behavior escalates to include money concerns. He accuses me of spending all his money. Since we married in 1990, Bob has been in charge of investing the money from my psychology practice after writing out the practice bills and paying our personal bills from our joint account. We do the receivables from my psychology practice together each month. I print out the bills on the computer and he folds, addresses, stamps and mails them. I enter the payments in the computer and he tallies the checks and makes the deposits. He also records the payables as I hate to write out checks. He reconciles the personal checkbook and tallies the tax preparation for the accountant.

Because Bob is complaining about our expenditures, I take out the checkbooks for the first time in many months. Some bills have not been paid. Others have been paid twice. There are charges on our account for fees which have never been there before. The balance on the last bank statement shows thousands of dollars in the checking account, but the checkbook had not been reconciled and the page tallies had not been made.

Bob quietly states, "I can't add the columns properly anymore, even with the adding machine tape. I'm getting different sums each time, even after three tries."

Now I understand better the possible reasons behind my husband's anger, and even his taking it out on me. After all, I am the closest person to him. But the rage behavior is something else. I suffered through a volatile marriage. I was living alone with my three children for eighteen years before I met Bob. One thing I promised myself is that I would never be subject to verbal abuse again.

After the episode in the attorney's office, Mrs. G. advises me to keep a journal, documenting my expenses and the progress of my husband's illness. I become once again a diligent student. I experience the journal as homework, a duty I have been asked to undertake for the future protection of my financial interest should someone question my assuming responsibility for our household finances. In the winter of 2009 I enroll in a short story writing class, the first creative writing class I ever experienced. Until now, my writing has been limited to psychology reports, progress notes for my patients and preparation for teaching other therapists about play therapy with children.

My first husband was a salesman, and as such he was attentive to the sales pitch of others who sold things. My first career was teaching elementary school children, so I have always listened carefully to teachers. Amy Dominy, the writer of young adult fiction who taught a short story writing course in Tempe, Arizona, taught me about character, scene and dialogue. She provided writing prompts and assignments. I thought I was keeping my mind alert and getting some respite from caregiving. When Bob and I returned to New York, my friends Marilynn and Sandy encouraged me to enroll in a writer's course at the YMCA where there is a group called The Writer's Voice. I met a memoirist, Mindy Lewis, who encouraged me to write in the first person about

4

my life. As I began to write, I realized that the burden of caregiving is a challenge far greater than any I have previously undertaken and that I would have to write about it in order to understand myself better, to be able to cope with the awful progress of this disease which no one will name for me.

All of a sudden it dawns on me, that I have lost my confidant; my life is empty, I am tired, I feel drained because I am lost in despair. By writing, I feel able to go on with my life. I feel that I may be able to help others who find themselves in a similar position, caring for a beloved spouse who is progressing through the maze of Alzheimer's disease or similar mind-stealing dementias. Describing the initial phases of memory loss may get someone to choose to get themselves or their loved one evaluated sooner. The process by which I determined to keep my husband as independent and as healthy as I could for as long as I could might give others courage as they travel through the maze of the health care system. As I share my feelings as a wife honestly, I may help other caregivers accept their complicated feelings as well. I also share who my husband was and what we had as a couple, so that the reader will be able to walk through this part of our lives with me and understand the immense loss that I feel.

2 – Initial Symptoms of Memory Loss

Chester, New Jersey, early November 2003

"I'm ready to sell the house."

The leaves have fallen. They cover the ground among the trees in a soft layer of brown, gold and beige. The sky is grey, the branches of the maples, oaks and sycamores deep brown and grey, strong and tall. From our vantage point in the second floor bedroom of our home in Chester, New Jersey, my husband and I look out at our patio, lawn and the copse of woods beyond. We have recently celebrated our anniversary, "thirteen good ones" my husband wrote on the sentimental Hallmark card. We stand together, connected at the hip and elbow, quietly, until I murmur, "It is so beautiful and peaceful here, even in the late fall and winter." I expect a "Mmmmm."

What I hear instead is, "Didn't you hear me?" Bob waits until I ask, "What did you say?"

"This is not fun anymore. Look at all the branches that have fallen. I'll have to collect them and cut them for kindling. What I see are more dead trees and branches in the woods. I'll have to cut them up and split the logs for firewood. The driveway needs another load of gravel. The gutters have to be cleaned of all the leaves."

Can I have heard him correctly? This house has been my husband's home for thirty-six years. He designed it, supervised its construction, and completed several of the rooms with his own hands. Here he and his first wife raised three children. Bob stayed on after the kids had grown and their mother died. The house is filled with his memories as well as his collections, his cookbooks, his knives, his tools, his stones, (each marked with the date and place he found it).

Leave this house? Why then had he bought a new electric saw for projects he intended to take on? And what would we do with the stuff we (basically he) have accumulated? They'd never fit into the small apartment we keep in New York.

What's more, I too have grown attached to the house. Together, Bob and I made changes to it - adding a sunroom with floor to ceiling windows, two decks and a wine room. My rattan porch furniture sits on his carpet in the sunroom. We updated the kitchen and the bathrooms, added the patio I am looking at, planted all that pachysandra.

Sell this house? Surely Bob can't be serious. But what if he is?

"I guess if you want to, you should," I say. I leave it to him to do what must be done, if he's going to follow through with this sale. A few weeks later, Bob tells me that we're to meet with a realtor and sign some papers. We're putting the house on the market. Having done some research on prices being asked for comparable homes in the neighborhood, Bob sets our asking price high because this house does have a high emotional value for us. Like the ad says, *it's priceless.* At any rate, after six months it doesn't sell and we take it off the market. *Okay with me.*

It is February, 2004. Bob, who has always been very generous to his children, forgets to send his son Adam a check and a card for his birthday. I remind him. In June, he forgets to send his firstborn daughter Alison her birthday gift. I buy a card and leave it for him where Bob writes out the checks. In August, before we leave for our vacation, I remind him that his middle child, Lauren's birthday is coming up. Small matters for sure, but Bob feels I am reminding him about many things he routinely handles.

"Stop nagging me about stuff!" he tells me.

My ears perk up. This is the first time Bob has ever spoken crossly to me. What we have is an honest to gosh love story, which neither of us expected to find. All we each wanted was not to be alone. Bob and I met through an ad Bob had placed in the personals column of The Jewish News. This was of course before online dating.

"Gentleman, age 60, desires the companionship of a woman who also likes travel, reading, foreign films, good food and wine; seeking a lasting relationship. Please respond to P.O. Box 1234, Ironia, N.J."

I answer it. We speak several times before we schedule a Sunday brunch at a New Jersey diner, situated halfway between his suburban home and mine. Here's what happens: I arrive early, sit in my Mercedes, dressed in my sweat suit after an aerobics class. The heater is on; it is February 2, 1989. I want to see him first as we haven't exchanged photos. *What will he be like in person?*

I see a red Nissan Sentra pull up. A man appears, dressed in an L.L. Bean parka that's way too big for him. *I hope that's not him, he's short.* I wait a few minutes, and then I make a grand entrance into the diner. Of course it is he. Bob welcomes me with a warm smile. Two hours later, brunch is finished and we go our separate ways. He says he will call. I drive home, not knowing whether I want him to call or not. Perhaps we could be friends. He's very easy to talk to, but he *is* short. That's not so bad if his clothing would be tailored to his size. He has such beautiful twinkling blue eyes. I have always been a sucker for blue eyes. And he has a cute little moustache and a goatee. His full head of wavy hair is brown, but his facial hair is white. He'd really be good looking if he let his hair grow a little longer and got some spiffy clothes. I phone my Aunt Lisa for a consult. She says, "Phyllis, your first husband was six foot two. That worked?"

Bob phones the next day. I invite him to dinner. He arrives at 6, eats the vegetarian dinner I have prepared and by 8:30, he leaves. *Why?* When he telephones the next evening I don't ask, but we set up a whole day date for Saturday. We spend the day in New York, in Greenwich Village, having coffee and biscotti, wandering the streets, telling each other about our lives, then stopping in Little Italy for a spaghetti dinner. He tells me he left early Tuesday because he had another date for later on that evening, and he had to tell Arlene he was no longer interested in her.

Bob has been open and direct with me. "I am so glad I found you," he says almost daily, delighted in a treat I have brought home or tickets I have purchased, or just happy to be looking at me. And now he doesn't want me to remind him to send his kids birthday checks?

Bob calls his children and says he will no longer be sending checks or even cards for their birthdays. *Okay; something is wrong.* Bob agrees to hire a gardener to mow the lawn, but complains that they only do "the easy parts". There is still trimming to be done and weeding between the flagstones on the patio.

We buy a shed from Ace hardware, painted grey with white shutters to match the house. It was built by the Amish and delivered from Pennsylvania in October, as this is the month when the young men have finished their summer projects and get married. The shed arrives on the back of a truck, driven by one man. His truck has a hydraulic lift. The driver asks where the back corner of the shed is to be placed, and directs the lever to place the shed exactly on the spot. Then he lowers the shed and removes the carrier base, like easing a pizza off the hot stone. We are amazed. Bob is so happy. The shed will house a small generator so we won't be without power when the winter storms knock down trees in our neighborhood. Bob makes shelves for the shed and moves in his garden hoses, his potting soils, his clay pots and small trowels, hoes and spades. Bob makes the shed a part of his enjoyment of the house. I am sure he wants to stay.

We travel to Europe for the month of August, as usual, exchanging our New York apartment this summer for a beach house in La Antilla, on the southern coast of Spain. Bob has made the arrangements. We have a wonderful trip. The beach house is spare, but clean. We stroll on the main street in the evening with the other older couples. We sleep late and eat late dinners. We rent a car and drive to Seville, staying in a small hotel near the cathedral and learning about the city. We have a wonderful, romantic adventure on the Isle of Gibraltar. The Rock Hotel is right out of a 1940's movie. It is cut into the rock and overlooks the sea. At night, all of the ships' lights are ablaze, necklaces of light strung across the harbor.

Then we return. Summer is over.

"Phyllis," Bob says, "I want help selling this house. I'm really serious. The workload is too much for me. I am having trouble remembering to do routine maintenance."

I still don't get it, but I agree. We hire another realtor, a neighbor of a friend of mine, who is a real go-getter. She helps me "stage" our house for sale. We remove many belongings to make the rooms look bigger. She has a video made and advertises on the web. Meanwhile, I am trying to understand what is happening. I tell my friend Adele that Bob wants to sell the house because he has trouble remembering. She commiserates and says she's feeling vulnerable herself, misplacing items she routinely uses. She suggests we read Dr. Andrew Weill's, "The Better Brain" book. I buy a copy. Following Weill's advice, we purchase seventeen different herbs and supplements for Bob to take daily to help his memory.

I don't want our lives to change. My practice is going well. I love having a country house and a small New York apartment. I love my husband who shares all of my interests and has so many of his own. But it is reasonable to sell the big house. We don't need it anymore. Bob has all of the responsibility for its upkeep. Most of his friends have sold their homes and moved to Florida.

By the end of the following summer, the house is finally sold. We are in Lisbon on the day of the closing. We get a telephone call just before dinner, which of course is very late in Lisbon. We ask the concierge of our Baixa hotel to recommend the best, most romantic restaurant in the neighborhood. He makes a reservation for us. We dress in our single travel dress outfits and we walk to an ordinary-looking office building. It is after business hours; the building looks deserted, so we're a bit skeptical as we ride the elevator to the seventh floor and enter a lovely, dark-paneled room, with one glass wall, and a balcony overlooking the old town of Lisbon with its Castle of Sao Jorge basking in the glow of amber light on the hill. So lovely. Bob orders champagne, and three bottles are brought to the table. "We'll have the *Veuve Cliquot* yellow label brut," declares Bob, winking at me.

"And for your dinner? What can we prepare for you?" asks the waiter. "All of our dishes are cooked to order." He realizes for sure that we don't read Portuguese, don't speak a word of it, as a matter of fact.

"Let's have fish," answers Bob, looking at me for agreement. The waiter leaves and returns with the chef, who, dressed in white, with a toque on his head, carries

12

a platter of three raw fish. We choose the turbot. We dine royally, thrilled that we have accomplished this two year goal.

When we return, it is to our apartment in the city. We bought this apartment in 2002. When Bob retired, in 1993, we rented an apartment and office duplex in a part of downtown Manhattan called Chelsea, right across 14th Street, in Greenwich Village where I had always wanted to live. It is a cute space in the back of the building. Our apartment is on the first floor; there is a door to a small backyard garden which one of the neighbors tends lovingly. The apartment has one large room, a kitchen nook and a wrought iron spiral staircase leading downstairs to my office. My patients have a separate entrance. We had decorated it all in IKEA, with Bob building all the hardwood pieces from the kits that we had picked up in Bob's Subaru station wagon. We lived in that apartment unfolding the sofabed, on Tuesdays and Wednesdays, for several years. But then Bob wanted to be on the Upper West Side of Manhattan. He wanted to own a space, not rent, in a more stable neighborhood. He also didn't like the pizza parlor in the front of the building. I think he might have seen rodents in the garbage collection room.

The building we move to has a roof deck with an herb garden which Bob utilizes in his food preparations. We sit on the Adirondack chairs in the evening and watch the sailboats and barges on the Hudson River, fireworks on the river on the Fourth of July. We share wine and cheese with our neighbors. The marble lobby with its brass doors and fittings is impressive. The 24 hour doormen are extremely helpful and friendly. Acting as our own contractors, we renovate the old kitchen. Our IKEA furniture fits, but we add a dining table and an enclosed home office unit. I change my office days, Monday and Thursday in the city, Tuesday and Wednesday in New Jersey, so we now spend our weekends with friends in the city.

We have lived this comfortable life for ten years. We have exchanged the apartment for other homes in Europe in addition to these past summers in Spain and Portugal. Now that we have sold the house, the apartment feels confining. I was using the bedroom as an office, folding and unfolding our futon. Bob was out and about, attending movies and museums during my office hours, having lunch with some of his relatives and friends. So now I rent office space nearby two days each week and spend two days commuting to New Jersey to my psychology practice. Bob still goes to museums, to shop, or to movies alone or with me. More and more I notice that Bob goes out less and less. He has nothing to tell about his day. This busy, active man is just sitting, reading, napping mostly, and doing essentially nothing. He has no interest in planning our next year's European trip. *I guess he's depressed. I knew that selling the house would be hard for him.*

He no longer wants to take the memory pills each day.

"The pills are not helping," he says. What he's telling me is that he's still experiencing memory problems, but I choose not to hear it. I want to believe that he's merely depressed, which will improve with time.

Bob decides to accompany me to New Jersey each week and we settle into a routine. We stay every Tuesday night in the same extended stay hotel with a kitchenette, in the town where Bob's best friend Eliot lives. I drop him off at Eliot's apartment at noon on Tuesday before my office hours begin. Bob spends the day with Eliot. Eliot and Ronnie, Bob and I have dinner together each week. The next morning, Bob drops me off at the office after breakfast and drives off to do whatever he wants for the day. He goes to the large stores where we used to shop and to the dentist; he does the banking, gathers groceries for the week and picks me up when my office hours are over. I reassure myself the plan is working.

One evening, Bob asks me to drive home. I think nothing of it. We have always shared driving. Bob had a car accident a few years earlier in which he broke his arm, and he worries about having another one.

But then he says, "I don't feel safe driving anymore."

"Not even when you are by yourself?" I ask. "Not even in the daytime?"

"I've decided. I'm not driving anymore." Bob has made up his mind.

"What are you going to do all day?" I ask.

"I'll stay in the waiting room," he says cheerfully.

Now I'm scared. Something is telling me things are going to get worse, not better and I will have to be available. I'll have to close the New Jersey practice. My priority is my husband.

For the rest of the school year, Bob sits in my New Jersey office waiting room every Tuesday and Wednesday. He reads the paper and walks across the street to buy us lunch. He walks to the bank or to the post office and chats with the people in the building. He also chats with my patients, mostly the parents of children in my practice. This is not tolerable in a psychologist's office. My patients understand that I need to refer them to other therapists so I can care for him. They sense that something is not quite right. Sadly, I part from my patients.

That summer, Bob and I fly to Denver to visit old friends who have retired. During our trip our friends ask what kind of food we want to eat. Bob has no preference. Where would we like to go? What would we like to see? Joel, who builds and flies model airplanes, has planned an outing to the flying field.

"Bob, let's get up early tomorrow and go flying. We'll catch breakfast out with the guys," he suggests.

"I don't think so," Bob answers, "I'll just stay here and do whatever Phyllis is doing."

"Phyllis," my friend Barbara asks, "Didn't Bob want to come on this trip? He doesn't seem to want to do anything."

They are correct. I do notice that Bob is not making any decisions. Through their eyes I come to see how dependent Bob has become on me for everything. They show me that he is counting on me to decide where to go, what to eat. When we return to the city in September, I decide it is time to see a neurologist.

3 – First Neurology Consults

New York, September 2006

I do want Bob to see a neurologist... and I don't. Whatever it is that my husband is dealing with; I am frightened of having someone put a name to it.

Clearly, there's enough cause for concern. For a while now, Bob has been experiencing difficulty in remembering what he did yesterday or earlier that same morning. *Normal aging?* He searches for words, resorting to phrases when a noun proves elusive. "Where's the thing you cut with?" he will ask me and I hand him the scissors. *A senior moment?* He has trouble following the story lines of favorite television programs. *Is this a hearing or a memory problem?* We are both worried, but we do not talk about what's troubling us. I find myself crying at the mere mention of anything sad or frustrating – not like me at all! My digestion is upset, I have trouble sleeping, am kept awake by memories of my mother who struggled with Alzheimer's disease, and fear that my husband will hear the same diagnosis. But I've also read that there are medications (unavailable in my mother's time) that, if started in the early stages of the disease, can slow its progression. I don't want to lose my husband. It's time for us to find out what we're dealing with.

All of our medical connections are in New Jersey where we lived. Though we've been in our Upper West Side place for five years, four of those years had us shuttling back and forth between our house and the city apartment. We have a New York internist, Dr. A., so I phone his office and schedule an appointment. I am hoping for an evaluation and for some direction.

When we see the doctor, almost immediately he starts typing notes into his computer while I describe the reasons that have brought us to his office. Click, click. He does not look up at us, but says aloud as he types, "Asks for referral to a neurologist. I concur."

"Yes," I say, "and who do you recommend?"

"I don't know anyone personally who does this work," he answers. "Look up the receiving hospital for your zip code, then check your health insurer's online directory and choose a neurologist affiliated with that institution."

So that was that.

The neurologist I find is in a neighboring zip code – ten blocks away from our home. Her credentials seem fine; in addition to her practice she teaches at the renowned medical college affiliated with Mount Sinai Hospital. I schedule an appointment.

When we arrive at her office, Bob is given a form to fill out.

Name: He signs his name.

Address: "I don't know our new address," Bob says.

We have been living in this apartment for five years. I tell him our address.

Today's date: Bob looks at me. I tell him.

He hands me the clipboard on which the form rests. "It's easier for you to do it," he says.

A small, thin woman comes to the entrance of the waiting room and calls Bob's name. She smiles warmly and introduces herself as Dr. M. A good sign. She shows us to a narrow office, painted a dull grey, and takes a seat behind a large metal desk, which is placed horizontally across the space. We sit in two chairs facing her desk. The only decorations in the room are several framed certificates hanging high on the wall, the print too small for me to read. The grey colors and the distance between the doctor and us reduce the positive feeling of her smile.

Dr. M. looks at Bob and says, "So how can I help you today?"

Bob does not answer. She turns her head in my direction. "Could you please tell me why you are here?" I play along. She knows why we are here. I sent her a full explanation when I set up the appointment.

"We are here because my husband is having some problems with his memory which are making him depressed," I say.

"Okay," she says as she turns her head once more. "Bob, I am going to ask you some questions. Will you answer my questions, please?"

"Sure," he shrugs.

The doctor begins, "What day is it today?"

Bob looks at me. "Wednesday?" he asks. He is not correct.

"Do you know the date?" she continues.

"I don't bother with those. I can look at the New York Times to see the date anytime I want to know it. And I can look at my watch to see the time."

19

Dr. M. asks, "What kinds of things did you do before these symptoms began?" Bob replies, "I read. I watch the news."

My husband has lost the concept of "before" and "after". He relates only in the present tense. Also, he doesn't realize he has "symptoms". Most of the time he will not admit that he has memory loss. He does not say that he has not heard the question. He often insists that I or someone else has not spoken clearly. He is not co-operating with the doctor, so I provide the information.

"Bob always loved going to museums and seeing foreign films," I tell her. "He read the reviews, selected the movies and generally critiqued the films afterwards. Almodovar has until recently been his favorite director. Bob loves classical music; Mozart and Beethoven, but not the modern composers. We have season tickets to the Philharmonic and attend the opera." I look at Bob as I speak hoping for a smile or a comment. Bob is looking at the doctor.

"What did you do before you sold your house?" Dr. M. asks Bob, looking directly at him. Bob tells the story of the day the house closed, the restaurant story, complete with champagne. Dr. M. listens quietly. I feel compelled to add to his account. I want her to know who he was, what he has already lost, what I am afraid of.

"My husband had a basement workshop with a bench saw and a table saw," I say. "He had so much scrap wood and hand tools, if he ever wanted to make or fix anything; he had all the parts he needed. Upstairs, Bob had a sewing room where he shortened his own sleeves and hemmed his pants. He gardened, shopped,

20

read recipes, and cooked. My husband is a collector. He owns 1000 cookbooks. He has a stamp collection and a foreign coin collection. He has been happily retired for ten years."

Bob adds, "I don't do that anymore. It was getting to be too much for me. I don't drive anymore either. No one had to tell me. I just knew it was time for me to stop driving."

Turning toward me, Dr. M. says, "I think you made a mistake selling your house. Your husband is now stuck here in the city where he has no opportunity to do the things he can still do. All that is left for him are cerebral activities. At the house he could do manual tasks for which he still has skills. He needs to have his sewing machine back. Where are his 1000 cookbooks?"

I begin to feel woozy. Does the doctor blame me for Bob's memory loss? Does she think I made him sell the house? I am ready to cry. Is she saying that his decline is my fault?

I am in a daze as we leave the office. Dr. M. directs us to go to the hospital for an MRI of my husband's brain and to return when she has obtained the results. At the next appointment, the neurologist decides that my husband "probably has some sort of dementia" based on a one per cent shrinking of my husband's brain, and prescribes the most common medication, Aricept. Of course I have heard of it, I've seen the ads touting it to be helpful for Moderate Alzheimer's disease. She doesn't say Alzheimer's disease, but I hear it. *I feel devastated. My worst fears are coming true. What is happening to Bob, to us? How will I cope with this? I am getting paid back for being so happy. Am I being punished for letting my sister Sharyn carry the burden of caring for my mother when she struggled with this disease?*

The medication makes Bob dizzy, which gives me hope. If it doesn't work, I reason, maybe Bob doesn't have the disease. When we return to Dr. M.'s office, however, she says that dizziness is a common reaction but she still changes the medication to another one in the same chemical group, Razadyne. Bob tolerates the initial dosage of the new medication well. During October and November, his mood improves. We attend two Philharmonic concerts. We have dinner with friends. Bob tells old jokes, as he used to.

The second medication is working. *Good. Maybe this is all depression? Can the new meds be effective so soon? Perhaps this is a placebo effect.* There have been studies which show patients can feel better if they just think they are being treated for an ailment.

We are going to Arizona to visit my children and grandchildren for Thanksgiving. Generally, my husband has always been anxious before a plane trip. We leave early.

"Do I have to take off my shoes AND my belt?" he asks as we are standing in line at security. Once we are through the screening, we find the gate and sit to wait.

Bob says, "I feel dizzy."

"Maybe that's because we didn't eat breakfast. Let's get something to eat." I respond pragmatically. "Just get your medications out of your backpack and we'll get some food."

"I already took my medications at home," says Bob.

Bob has diabetes and takes a time-released medica-tion to help him digest food. It has to be taken with food, and Bob hasn't eaten. Of course he's dizzy. We buy him some food. He eats. He's quiet. Bob is generally an emo-tionally passive man, not prone to complaining unneces-sarily. I think the dizziness will pass.

Our plane arrives, our row is called, we board and are seated. The doors are closed and we are taxiing on the runway. Suddenly Bob rings the bell for the flight attendant.

"What can I get for you?" she asks.

"I have to get off this plane," he says in consterna-tion. "I'm dizzy. I can't stay on this plane for four hours." The flight attendant tells this to the airline crew. We return to the gate and are escorted from the plane.

I feel so embarrassed. My husband is not ill. A por-ter comes with a wheelchair. An ambulance screams onto the field. The medics haul out a stretcher, and oxy-gen. Bob refuses to get on the stretcher. He says the wheelchair is just fine. The medics check him out, kind-ly, and reassure us that his vital signs are good. Bob refuses to go to the emergency room, a decision I agree with. Instead, he goes to see Dr. A. when we get back home. The airline offers and books us seats for the fol-lowing day, with no penalty. I am grateful.

Dr. A. shakes our hands, sits down behind his desk, types into the computer which tells the doctor, and the doctor reads aloud to the patient, "In some cases the new medication, Razadyne, has been shown to be incompatible with the Lipitor you are already taking for high cholesterol."

The doctor smiles. He looks proud of himself. He feels he has explained the dizzy symptoms. I fume quietly. *This doctor has no clue. He doesn't know my husband or me. I understand he is going strictly by the computer.* Dr. A. is inconsiderate of my husband's condition and of his vulnerability. Patients of my husband's generation develop attachments to their physicians and trust them implicitly. Dr. A. sounds as if he were in competition with Dr. M. the neurologist; that he has discovered something she should have known. *Great, but don't destroy the neurologist's relationship with your patient unless you have an alternative to suggest!*

Bob says, "I'm not going back there again. She should have known the two medicines don't go together."

I knew that's what he would say. Dr. A. shrugs his shoulders.

"You went to NYU. Why don't you use a neurologist from there?" he says to me as he holds the door open for us to leave. *You went there, too, and you never gave me the name of a neurologist at NYU Medical Center when we asked.*

Bob is no longer dizzy. We take the plane trip the next day with no problems. The visit goes well. Bob helps with the preparation for Thanksgiving dinner. He cuts up veggies for the salad, and my daughter Linda asks him to make gravy, which he does every year. He's always carved the turkey, too. He even bought Linda new knives so she'd have them available for him to carve.

This time he hesitates, which is noticed by Linda's mother-in-law.

"Bob, here, let me help with that," Bobbie begins, "Let's get the flour and mix it with some water." She continues to guide him through the process for making gravy. Bob is so thankful; he mentions her help at dinner. Dave, Linda's husband, carves the turkey.

Bob cannot be depressed with a joyful grandson to play with. Grandpa Bob and Grant, who is not yet four, have such a good time together. The guest bedroom in my daughter's house is on the main floor, just off the family room. Grant comes downstairs early in the morning, dressed in his Sponge Bob pajamas, dragging his "white pillow", sits on his small love seat in front of the chaise end of the couches, and turns on his favorite Sponge Bob cartoons. These have been recorded previously and Grant knows how to locate and play each one. Grandpa Bob joins Grant and they play, as they watch and listen, getting out the toy cars and trucks, building roads and roadblocks on the floor. During the visit, Grant asks to sit next to Grandpa Bob every time we are in the car or at the table. They tease and thoroughly enjoy each other's company. Grandpa Bob doesn't reprimand or criticize. He just plays. Sometimes Grandpa Bob teases too much and they "fight". My daughter has to intervene.

When we get back to New York, I have to call Dr. M. and tell her what happened. Dr. M. is very understanding when I explain that Bob refuses to return to her practice because of Dr. A.'s statement that Dr. M. "should have known" the two medications were incompatible. She recommends a colleague. But now we have to travel to Mt. Sinai Hospital to see him. We find our way to the hospital, after taking a crosstown bus and an uptown bus.

"Why are we going to a hospital? Do I have to stay here? What are you DOING to me?" The hospital setting, the strangers in the large waiting room make Bob anxious.

We meet Dr. W. He's friendly, but he takes phone calls during our visit. The neurologist is a man in his fifties, with round glasses, a receding hairline and a ready smile. He doesn't wear a lab coat or a stethoscope. He tries to joke with my husband. He leads Bob into the examination room, checks his reflexes, his walking and his eye- hand control as well as his verbal interactions. He concurs with the first neurologist and prescribes a different medication, Namenda. Dr. W. advises us that medication might delay the process of memory decline somewhat, but is not a cure. He agrees that my husband has dementia, "but I don't think it is the bad kind." *Is there a good kind of dementia? Is he saying he thinks Bob doesn't have Alzheimer's disease, merely senility?* Dr. W. is personable, but he does not seem knowledgeable about dementia, to me at least. Dr. W. I find out, specializes in research at the hospital. He asks Bob to return for carotid artery testing. I think he needs subjects for his research. Bob does not need this test for any diagnosis. Bob refuses and the doctor graciously accepts the fact. Dr. W. says my husband is depressed.

We already know that. Dr. W. does not know that my husband was less depressed when he thought he was receiving medicine that would help him. None of the doctors seems particularly interested in my husband's case. At 76 years of age, Bob is physically healthy. His diabetes and his cholesterol levels are under control. His short term memory is gone.

Lots of long term memory is also missing, or at least Bob is unable to retrieve the information when needed. He is unable to make decisions. He is anxious, fearful of the future within the next few minutes.

"Are you sure he said we could go?" Bob hesitates when leaving the office, fearing even this change.

No physician mentions Alzheimer's disease. The medical profession hesitates to label as a disease something they cannot prove exists. Right now, the only proof of Alzheimer's disease is found on autopsy. And no one has any advice to give us on how to live, forget live well, with this non-diagnosis of a disease which is not going to get better and no one can tell when and how it will get worse.

What happens to me when I hear the diagnosis for the first time? Part of me feels vindicated. I am right. There really is something wrong with my husband. It is not my imagination. Bob has been complaining for months that I don't put things away in the same place each time, blaming me for his inability to find things. This memory loss cannot be my fault, yet, I feel guilty.

Bob noticed that he was forgetting to do the routine maintenance of the house, forgetting to call the oil company for a delivery, not scheduling snow removal. I didn't. We lived with that knowledge for the two years it took to sell the house. By selling the house, we made life easier for him. He can now walk to take his shirts to the tailor to have the sleeves shortened. He doesn't need to do them himself. He doesn't have to worry about ice forming between the shingles and the walls of the house during the winters.

Should we have sought a neurology consult earlier? Should he have been taking prescription medication sooner? The doctor said the change from the house to the apartment full time was bad for him. He needed a workroom. Now he no longer had cognitive capability.

After I begin to understand the diagnosis, I start to see his illness differently. Up till now, we have always figured things out together. Now I have to analyze everything myself. Whether it has something to do with just Bob or with both of us; the decisions will all be mine now. I have been responding emotionally, focusing on him, but also on me. How am I going to deal with this change in our lives? How will we manage? How will we cope? How can I figure out everything on my own?

I realize, after some research of my own, that Namenda, the medication that my husband has just been prescribed, has a specific usefulness. It is not like Aricept, which is touted to slow the progress of Alzheimer's disease. Namenda increases on-task performance. That means Bob could finish something he starts. If he starts making a salad, for example, the Namenda can help him stay with the salad job until it is finished, not leave the kitchen with the salad ingredients cut up, but spread all over the counter. The medication does not return to him skills he already lost.

One day Bob buys a large can of crushed tomatoes at the grocery store. He says as he unpacks it, "Next time we have spaghetti, I am going to make sauce. I don't know where to find how to do it, but I will."

That night I cook spaghetti for dinner. Bob watches me make the sauce and when I ask him to, Bob adds the spices, choosing garlic, oregano, salt and pepper. He completes a project I start. He does not remember buying the tomatoes; it does not matter. This is a cooperative venture. Together we enjoy the results of our joint labor.

The medication does not return to him interests that are no longer there. He is no longer able to follow the story on television or in the theater. So he is no longer interested in reading movie reviews, but he still recognizes the old movie stars. I record old movies for us to watch. We watch nature stories and science stories and the history channel now.

I ponder ways to make Bob's environment work for him. We need projects he can do to make him feel useful and needed. In order to accomplish this, we need more room than we have in our one bedroom apartment. I make an appointment with the realtor who sold us the small apartment and ask to be shown a larger space. We see eight different apartments in one day and choose one, settling on a March closing. That gives us all winter to sell our smaller apartment.

It's impossible to "stage" this apartment for resale. I do buy rolls of cookie dough. Before every open house, I slice and bake chocolate chip cookies and leave them on the table. Sometimes the realtor schedules an appointment during my office hours. Bob refuses to leave the apartment at those times. For one thing, there is no longer any place he is comfortable to go by himself. For another, the weather is cold which adds to the problem. Bob fights with the realtor.

"You let those people leave without even talking to them," Bob tells the agent one day.

"How do you know they weren't interested?" Bob challenges the agent.

"I have a real estate license." (He once did.) "I never sold a house, but I know how it is supposed to be done."

Bob interferes. He takes over, showing prospective buyers and their agents his collection of cookbooks. Visitors are eager to leave. The agent might quit as well. Luckily, by springtime, a fellow resident expresses interest in buying our apartment. We are saved.

We close on the new apartment in March. Will the old apartment close on time? Will the renovations be complete in time for the closing? All of this is now mine alone to deal with. Bob is not interested. I take out our money from our retirement funds, which have to be replaced within 60 days. Fortunately we close on the old apartment in time to put the money back. I encounter troubles with the co-op board, problems with the new superintendent who wants the contract to repaint and finish the floors, but offers an estimate which is almost double the going rate. There are delays in starting to renovate the new space. Finally in June, Bob has a workroom, and his sewing machine back.

We have to move in before the kitchen renovation is completed. The appliances in the kitchen are beyond cleaning. All must be replaced. A change of location can be confusing to any of us; it is certainly the case with someone suffering from dementia. The familiar is reassuring, the new is threatening. Bob is very confused at moving time. He despises disorder, now more than ever.

"Why is the new refrigerator sitting in the living room?" he wants to know.

"We just bought a new apartment," he says when he remembers. "Why are we eating out all the time?" Bob gets angry about spending so much money on breakfast and diner lunches.

We retrieve my grandparent's dining room set and all the heirlooms that are displayed in the breakfront, from storage in New Jersey and donate our IKEA furniture to charity. We purchase new bedroom furniture. We move the cookbooks from the New Jersey storage to Sophia Storage on Amsterdam Avenue, three blocks from our new apartment. The new apartment is seven street blocks and four avenue blocks from the old apartment. We were closer to the Hudson River and its waterfront park. Now we are one block from Central Park.

Bob has a new destination and another task to complete. He will sort and decide which cookbooks to sell, which to donate and which to keep. He has the lock and key as well as new clean boxes which Tony, the building handyman, saves for him. He has his markers and his masking tape. Bob can walk to the storage unit alone. Francis, who works there, and I have a pact. Francis is very helpful, taking Bob up to the fourth floor on the freight elevator, and checking on him frequently. Bob is not happy if he sees me tip Francis. "It's just part of his job to be helpful," he grumbles.

Bob sorts and re-boxes his books. We sell or donate more than 600 books, using the car to transport the boxes to the Strand Book store or to Housing Works, an upscale thrift book store on Crosby Street. There are too many for the local thrift store to accommodate. Four hundred more books remain in storage. Bob is unwilling to part with them. We have no more room to house them. We have already created two walls of bookcases in Bob's hobby room, eleven feet long and nine feet high.

Meanwhile Bob decides to place quarter round molding along the edges of all of the floors in our 1100 square foot apartment, as he did in the small apartment several years ago. He walks to the lumber store to buy the molding. He chats with the workmen at the store. He buys a new miter box. He has his hand saws, one of which has his father's name painted on it. It is a real antique. He asks the painters to leave him some paint for the molding before he attaches it.

After this job is complete, he strips all of the old paint from the front door, using a torch. He refinishes the door. He removes each of the brass doorknobs and jams from the eleven closet and room doors, cleans, shines and replaces them. He transforms the second closet in his room for tools. He builds narrow shelves on one side and wider shelves on the other side. He moves his tools into the closet, along with enough light bulbs to last for a few years, extension cords, a shoe shine kit and briefcases full of stamps.

I feel proud of his accomplishments – and mine. The move has enabled Bob to have dignity, to feel useful, to accomplish important tasks. No longer depressed, Bob looks forward to each day. Some nights he doesn't want to stop working to go to bed. But if I am going to bed, he is happy to join me there.

We change our travel plans, but we do not stop traveling. We join a college alumnae tour to India. We have no decisions to make, no luggage to carry. We travel with a group; we are impressed by the beauty of the *Taj Mahal* and the squalor of the people who live near it. We are entertained by a Maharajah and by a Brahmin military officer and his family. Bob buys me two lovely bangle bracelets and a ring to celebrate our journey and we enjoy ourselves immensely. Although Bob has kept a record of all our trips before this one, there is no journal of this trip.

During the winter, our New York Philharmonic Orchestra seatmates talk of traveling without a tour group to Russia. We decide next summer, we will travel, two couples together, to St. Petersburg for the White Nights and to Moscow. Bob reads about Peter the Great. He gets a huge book of Russian history and I begin to relax.

4 – So What IS Normal Aging?

New York, 2006

I need to know more about aging, what's normal, what isn't, so I look for models to guide me. I remember listening to a lecture by the famed behavioral psychologist, B.F. Skinner, about his own aging. He described being able to do everything he was accustomed to do, but in shorter time periods, interspersed with rest. He implied that other limitations besides time spent on any one activity would be abnormal. I know many New Yorkers, people well into their eighties, a few who are in their nineties and two women who are over 100 for whom this is a valid description. Some who have arthritis state that their days of activity are sometimes limited by pain. Some are cancer survivors. Others tell me: "I'm not the person I was." When asked to explain, they list a slowing of interests in attending lectures, plays and concerts. Where they were accustomed to four events per week, they settle for two or maybe three. They report sometimes, regretfully being sidelined by bad weather, either cold or hot, rain and snow.

Some folks I interviewed suggest that their interests are changing as they age. They watch the History Channel, Animal Planet, or the Discovery Channel and are no longer interested in dramas and sit-coms on television. Attendance at movies is decreased as well, except for movies that can be watched at home and suspended if necessary, or rewound and repeated. One woman has become an *aficionada* of reruns of "Law and Order". She wears two hearing aids and walks with a cane after two hip surgeries.

I, too, forget things – like acknowledging people's birthdays and returning phone calls. Twice I double-booked appointments. Normal or not?

These things happen to us all. But we get much more upset about them as we age. Some people like us have "downsized" their homes, moving to apartments in doorman buildings in the city, selling their suburban homes as we did. These people may joke of having "a senior moment." The kind of memory loss my husband is experiencing is not a part of normal aging. Older folks continue to travel, mostly with tour groups where they formerly went with a friend or a spouse alone. They join Elder Hostel groups. They visit family and friends or they go on cruises. They meet friends and relatives in restaurants rather than entertain at home. And many eat more lightly. All of these things occur in normal aging.

A woman friend of mine, now 82, never married, lives alone in New York, still works a few days a week doing secretarial duties. A few weeks ago she was to meet with us and others at a friend's home for dinner. We all sat and waited for her. She never showed up. She has no cell phone, so we thought she was on her way. We ate without her. At 9 p.m., two and a half hours later, she telephones. She fell asleep and forgot to come. She woke up, looked at the calendar and remembered to call and make her apologies. If this were the beginning of dementia for her, she would soon cease to realize that she is forgetting. But the fact that she remembered to look at the calendar, recognized that she had fallen asleep and then called to make her apologies, suggests that this is indeed, normal forgetfulness. She may need to admit to herself that she needs more rest in her day and plan for it.

When folks are at the very beginning of memory loss, they know they are being forgetful and they know it is not normal aging. My husband knew when he was willing to sell his beloved house. Unfortunately, one hallmark of dementia is the person's inability to recognize the symptoms as a disease. Generally my husband Bob began to rationalize, to deny and to lie to himself. He told himself for example that he "decided" not to drive any longer, not that he was losing his memory or his judgment. Then, slowly, that awareness disappeared. That's because other cognitive deficits, other ways of thinking also become impaired. The first of these involves decision making. The boss of our thinking decides what we will do, feel, say, even chooses what we want to eat, when we want to sleep. Surely, we fall asleep without a decision when we are too tired to remain awake, but that requires no decision. We also eat whatever is served to us or for that matter, whatever is available, if we are very hungry. Bob started having difficulty deciding what he wanted to eat, when he wanted to sleep, what he wanted to do.

Some changes in memory older folks may experience as a normal part of aging occur in the areas of visual memory, verbal memory, immediate memory, working memory and episodic memory. Visual memory includes things like remembering where you left your glasses or your hearing aids. One woman I know keeps her hearing aids in a suede pouch on a suede cord around her neck tucked into her blouse. That way she always knows where they are and doesn't have to go rummaging through her purse. Unfortunately when Bob misplaces objects, he blames me for hiding them.

Verbal memory includes remembering "what's-his-name" the star of the movie you watched last night, while you still can recall the plot, characterization and point of the film. Bob always prided himself in his knowledge of people. He could recognize them by sight and could name them, from movie stars to colleagues and acquaintances. My visual memory has always been deficient. As I age it is progressively harder for me to remember the names of people I meet.

Immediate memory is the recall of numbers or letters you have just heard, before you type them into your cell phone. Since I have very good immediate memory, Bob has relied on me for telephone numbers and addresses, so I don't see the decline in his immediate memory. The ability to name objects sounds more drastic than it is. How often do we say, "Hand me that thing" when looking to change channels on the television set? But Bob is having more frequent problems finding the names of objects. He will define something by its function more often than is normal. "Hand me that thing you cover yourself with," he might say, pointing to a towel.

Working memory is the ability to hold on to small bits of recently learned information. When Bob cooked, he could read the recipe, gather the ingredients and then perhaps look again to see how they were to be cut, diced, sliced or grated. Then he did all of those before looking again to see how the ingredients were to be combined. He looked again to check on the length of time and the temperature required for cooking the item. Then he checked the recipe for spicing, perhaps, or the thickness of the sauce. Bob used to do all that. After the dish was completed, he would annotate the recipe, cut it out to place in his recipe notebook. Later, he would again go to the file, rate the completed product and note how to improve the recipe, or whether to bother making it again. Now he limits himself to recipes he knows how to prepare. He has favorites like Spanish Cod in Tomato Sauce with Olives that he prepares often.

He still reads recipes and saves them, but he has not tried new ones, so they sit inside the cover of one of his spiral notebooks.

My mother used the same kind of episodic or unconscious memory when baking. She "knew" how to make cookie dough. She had recipes to choose which cookie she was preparing, but the rest of the process was accomplished without checking any source. She sent a variety of cookies to each of her grandchildren when they were in college, placing each in mini-muffin papers, packaging the metal boxes tightly and shipping them off via the postal service. When the cookies began arriving crumbled, or missing an ingredient, the kids knew something was wrong. Grandma didn't. She was losing her episodic memory. My mother also "knew" how to play the piano. Long after she knew not much else, as she developed Alzheimer's disease, she could sit down "there" and "get music out if it". Snatches of Mendelssohn mostly, from what I could tell. She could not.

So, knowing all of this, I still was puzzled by my husband's behavior and his memory loss. As he began to lose his memory, Bob reduced his functioning altogether. He didn't get lost, he stopped driving. He didn't forget to gather small branches for kindling. He just didn't gather them anymore. He still cooked and cleaned the kitchen. He read the newspaper every day. He lost his ability to be independent, preferring to follow me around all day. My presence oriented him in time. His main deficit was a loss of a sense of time, an inability to plan for the future, even when the future was to happen soon.

"What should we cook for dinner tonight?" asked by me, was now followed by his response "I'm not hungry." In the beginning I would say," We can't wait to cook until we *are* hungry, can we?" Bob just shrugged his shoulders.

He can no longer remember the groceries we bought or what is available for us to choose from for our dinners. So I begin to cook our dinners which are much simpler than Bob's recipes. We don't change our diet, as we have always followed the Mediterranean Plan, eating mostly fresh fruits and vegetables with some fish or seafood added. After Bob was diagnosed with Adult Onset Diabetes, we added chicken to our diet and reduced our pasta consumption.

In addition, it is sometimes the case in normal aging that personality issues arise; some curmudgeonly grumpy old men behaviors occur as skills diminish and interests decline. Most of these behaviors are directed towards beloved family members; unresolved conflicts are no longer hidden. What the older person feels and thinks often is directly expressed. Many times the issues concern money, especially since inflation has so increased the dollar numbers. A subway ride that cost a nickel, now requires $ 2.25.

Looking back, what we neglected to do was to get clearance from our physician before taking the supplements that were recommended by Dr. Weill's book and Dr. Perlmutter's book. Each author recommended getting a doctor's exam and authorization before consuming any supplements in large quantities. I worried that something was very wrong with my husband's memory. I felt that this was not normal aging. But it is so hard to confront even the possibility of such a devastating diagnosis that we didn't ask the questions. I hope that by writing this book, I can convince people to consult with a neurologist after visiting their primary care physician. Ask for brain imaging. It is very important to get what is called "baseline data." What does your brain look like now? How much if any shrinkage has already occurred? If Bob had an early neurological exam, including an MRI, a year later we would have been in a much better position to know if supplements worked, or if other dementia-slowing medication was indicated.

5 – Personality Changes

December 2007 – January 2008

Life was going so well, we decided to stay for two weeks in Arizona in December 2007. This time Grant wanted to shower with Grandpa Bob and watch him shave. Grandpa taught him how to put shaving cream on his face and to "shave" with a long, skinny Lego brick. My son Steve took Bob on outings, just the guys. Bob saw signs advertising go-go dancers and asked Steve to take him to a show; but to keep it a secret from Linda and me. They went to a girlie show in the afternoon, where young women were dancing almost nude. Bob asked to touch a black woman, to see, Steve reported, if she felt different from a white woman. This was such unusual behavior for my husband, which Steve recognized. Curious, however, Steve obliged him and paid for the woman to stand and talk with Bob. He asked to touch her arm. She agreed, and Bob smiled, pleased that he could feel no difference. Bob then spent 20 minutes (Steve had to pay $ 10.00 for each ten minutes) trying to dissuade the woman from her job, telling her she could be a visual model, or a clothing model, or even a print model. Bob remembered that adventure for days. He couldn't keep that secret for more than a half hour when they returned.

Bob was more interested in touching me, too, which was a source of anxiety for me, but I didn't deal with it. I accessed the online support group for spouses of Alz-

41

heimer sufferers, thealzheimerspouse.com, for advice and the spouses suggested I enjoy the touching while it was offered, as it would soon be forgotten, too.

Why did my husband's touch make me feel anxious? Because my expectations for a reciprocal relationship arose. We had an active loving sex life for many years. For almost two years now, my husband has not been able to maintain an erection. When he does occasionally have an early morning erection, it doesn't last long enough or isn't strong enough for penetration. We have given up, finding other ways to satisfy each other. After a while, Bob forgot what I like, so we substitute cuddle sessions, holding, and back rubs. Lately Bob isn't aware of me as a person separate from him. When he touches me, it feels much like a baby fondling a parent's arm or a soft blanket. The baby's touch is for the self-soothing of the baby. The baby's self-soothing is often accompanied by rocking. It needs to be held by the caregiver to feel safe. So it is now with my husband. The actual touch feels good to both of us, but if it is arousing to me, as it used to be, my touch would then arouse him further, thus making the touching reciprocal. No longer. My touch is experienced as soothing to him but not to me. He enjoys both touching me and me touching him, and he rolls over for a back rub and goes to sleep. I feel uncomfortable and alone. Over time, I begin to feel used by him. I know his behavior is not purposeful, he is not ignoring my needs on purpose, but logic doesn't control feelings. So when he comes near me in bed, I feel anxious. In the morning, I offer back rubs, hoping he will fall back asleep.

While we are in Arizona, everyone is discussing the real estate bust and how low prices have fallen. My daughter has wanted me to move to Arizona forever. "Now," she says, "is the perfect time to buy a retirement home." So, just for fun, Linda, Grant, Bob and I go house hunting. Linda is a real estate agent, so she's doing research for clients at the same time. It is school break, so Grant is available to join us. He is very funny, figuring out which room would be his, in our retirement home. Bob has a great time, too, evaluating the homes. Bob's expertise, of course, is telling everyone what is wrong with each house we see. He begins to know what he would like in a retirement home, a garage workshop and fruit trees in the back yard. We find a semi-attached villa in a retirement community, with an orange tree and a grapefruit tree in the back, with fruit ready for picking. Bob delightedly harvests some fruit. He sits contentedly on a patio looking out onto a golf course. The white stucco house is across the street from the community center. We explore a pool and a library. It is winter time, but there are two women swimming. Steve and Bob return the next morning to see the house again. They see the pool room in the community center; one group of guys is shooting pool and as it is Sunday morning, another group of men are preparing a pancake breakfast. This breakfast is a fund raiser for the community.

Bob quips, "Next year, one of you guys will move over, I'll be flipping some of those pancakes."

Bob decides to place a bid on the house, based on the asking price and on Bob's valuation of the fifteen year old home. Our bid is accepted just as it is time for us to return to the city. The paperwork follows us, by fax and Fed-Ex. Purchasing a home is simplified in Arizona as no lawyers are needed. Both the buyer and the seller split one real estate fee. Once the contract of sale is signed, a home inspection is ordered, the title is searched by the title company, the seller is obligated to fix what needs fixing and the closing happens.

The contract that arrives in New York has many places to initial and sign. Each page requires at least one set of signatures.

"Why do I have to sign here? How do I know I agree with what this says? You're not giving me enough time to read this. I won't sign anything unless I read it. Stop. Stop, STOP!"

We agree for the lawyer to look over the contract. Bob is extremely agitated for the first time ever. There's a confrontation in the lawyer's office, which ends peacefully, with Bob understanding our estate plan, and with our decision not to purchase the house. However, Bob does not stop being agitated and abusive. He becomes insulting and nasty. So I decide to call Bob's son. This is a difficult decision for me. Bob's son, Adam, the youngest of Bob's children, is a lawyer; Alison, the oldest is the director of traffic for a large mail order catalogue company and Lauren, the middle child, fifteen months younger than her sister, works as a securities salesperson for a large bank. They each are married and have children. They are busy; their lives are full. We see them seldom which seems to be the way they want it.

Adam's wife, Sheree, is the warmest and the one who is closest to me. She asks me questions about child rearing and includes me in the progress of the girls, but she, too, is limited by the distance her husband and his sisters maintain from us. I believe this is a result of the trauma which resulted from the death of their mother when they were in their twenties. Bob attended a bereavement group after his wife's death, but when Bob and I met, I encouraged him to attend individual therapy sessions for a year to help him process his grief and anger towards his deceased wife, who suffered from cancer, non-Hodgkin's lymphoma, which is now more manageable, but then carried a death sentence. I don't know what help his children received to help process their sense of loss and abandonment.

Bob's children and especially their spouses are cordial, visits proceed smoothly, and Bob and I are welcome to stay in their homes when we travel to see the grandchildren. Their attitude seems to change after Bob decides not to send them birthday cards or checks any longer and stops me from doing so for him. Now, the children have grown even more distant; they are unhappy with their father's decision to sell their childhood home. They see in his declining memory something worthy of blame; if indeed it is not his fault, surely it must be mine. So I have been alone dealing with my husband's illness; I speak with my children about him, but now that Bob is SO upset, I feel only his son could calm him.

"Adam, I need you to talk to your father. I need you to calm him down. He is ranting and raving. He's cursing and calling me names."

Adam answers, "I'm not surprised by my father's behavior. He always was a nasty person." I am floored. My husband never exhibited any angry behavior before 2003, and then he was irked, not rageful.

Adam continues, "If you can't take it anymore, I'll step up to the plate."

"What does that mean, Adam?" *I am not thinking straight.*

"Just divorce him, split your assets and I'll find my father an assisted living apartment near me." *Adam, you're a lawyer, but your wish for your father to be rid of me is getting in your way of caring about him.* He doesn't really know what he is offering. Assisted living apartments, where available in New Jersey have wait lists and are expensive. Bob's savings would be used up within a few years, and then where would he be? All alone? The burden of his care would fall on Sheree, Adam's wife.

"I'll think about what you said," I respond soberly. I end the conversation. Quietly I contemplate his offer. *Bob is not the father of my children. We have had 18 good years together. I don't have to take care of him through this long illness.*

I discuss Adam's proposal with his father. "Bob, I called Adam." Bob is angry. "Well, I called him first. I don't need you. I could live here at the apartment by myself without you or anyone else. I won't go to an assisted living apartment."

Then later, he says, "What does Adam want me to do?"

"Bob, this is your choice," I respond, "I will not live like this. I will not have you yelling at me. There is medicine available that will control your behavior if you cannot control it yourself. So choose, live here with me, go to an evaluation center for dementia and take medicine to control your behavior or go live in an assisted living facility in New Jersey."

"Where will you be?" he wants to know.

"Here in the apartment," I state.

"Alone?" he wonders.

"Yes, alone." I am calm, not smiling.

"I don't want to sleep alone." Bob looks like an abandoned child.

"So, what do you choose?" I feel ruthless.

"I choose you." Bob is very quiet.

I dial Adam's number. I put Bob on one extension and me on the other. "Adam, we have come to a decision. Bob, tell Adam what you have decided."

"Adam, what do you want me to do?" Bob asks.

"NO," I say firmly, "This is your choice and your choice only. Adam will do what you want him to do. What do you choose?"

"I choose you." Adam hears, asks no questions and we all hang up.

I take over the checkbook, preparing the information for the accountant at my office, so Bob doesn't have to see me do it. I research geriatric care clinics, and choose Mount Sinai's Martha Stewart Center. Other clinics for Alzheimer disease patients won't accept him, as my husband does not have Medicare. As a federal government retiree, Bob has a pension and health care insurance (we contribute about $ 400.00 monthly) but he was advised not to enroll in Medicare. Our first appointment at Mt. Sinai is February 15, 2008.

My expectations are that all the services my husband needs will be provided at one place. Medication interactions will be noted before an emergency situation arises. My need for the internist would no longer exist. Bob would receive neuropsychological testing, medication for cholesterol and blood sugar monitoring for diabetes on a quarterly basis. I expect to pay co-pays for each visit in addition to our yearly deductible. The reality is somewhat different.

The geriatrician is a young woman wearing a stethoscope around her neck to distinguish herself from the other young, competent women who draw blood, weigh and measure. All have pleasant attitudes, speak directly to the patient. There is no long wait time, either for an appointment or to be seen. The atmosphere is modern, the corridors and offices are painted in muted non- institutional colors.

But Mount Sinai Hospital doesn't accept our insurance and expects me to pay $ 200.00 for the hospital and $180.00 for the physician each visit. I decide to stay and pay. *I'll try it for a year. It has to be really great at these rates,* I figure. The geriatrician prescribes 0.5 mg Haldol for the agitation and orders a full battery of psychological tests. The psychologist happens to have a private office near our apartment. Bob can walk there by himself. The testing is paid 60% by the insurance company, 40% by us. The results of the testing indicate that Bob has Mild Cognitive Impairment. I am told the

48

diagnosis will change to Alzheimer's disease next year if a retesting indicates loss of cognitive functioning from this year's results, as well as if a new MRI shows further decrease in the size of my husband's brain. The psychologist also sees in the testing that my husband has depression and recommends talk therapy to deal with his issues. I know talk therapy doesn't work for demented patients, but Bob could use an outlet to vent his feelings, and a professional to allay his fears and help Bob stay focused. Dr. S. agrees to see Bob in treatment, which I like, as Bob knows him and can get to his appointments alone.

After six sessions, the psychologist calls me, stating, "I think we should discontinue the sessions, as your husband has no insight into his problems and no interest in their resolution." Bob is disappointed as he enjoyed the visits.

I can't believe this, either. Here is man in my own profession, expecting insight from a demented patient. He is refusing to treat him after only six sessions, even though Bob is talking to him.

Bob is calm. I don't know if it is the medication, as it is such a low dose. It might have been the therapy, but that didn't last long. Maybe it's the clinic. He likes coming here.

It's worth continuing at the clinic, I think.

But after the third and the fourth quarterly visit, I see that nothing is done. The blood work is ordered, but we have to go to the lab to have the blood drawn. They haven't received the MRI that was done in their own hospital. I have to go personally to Medical Records and pay $ 35.00 to get a disc for them. A new medical student interviews Bob each visit, in the same room with me and the physician. The physician is questioning me and listening to the student's interviewing skills progress at the same time. Between visits, Bob develops a cold, or perhaps allergy symptoms. He wants to see a doctor. When I phone, I am advised to return to our regular physician. We don't return to the clinic. We return to Dr. A, who agrees to write the prescription refills for the Haldol. To be fair, after our year's absence, Dr. A.'s office has changed. The front office staff is friendlier and Dr. A. seems to understand better, that I know what I am talking about and that this disease has both of us in a fragile state.

6 – I Need Help

We have all lost someone or something dear to us. When my big doll, Doris, was old and dirty, my mother said, "Phyllis, you can't play with her anymore unless someone fixes her." I cried and cried. I didn't want her fixed. I wanted my Doris. So what if her eyes were no longer attached and her blue and white checked apron was dingy grey. Her yellow curls hung from her wobbly cotton head. My Uncle Joey, well, he was not really my uncle, he was a soldier my parents befriended during the war; Uncle Joey stayed with us when he was on leave, as he was a refugee from Germany and he had no family in the United States. He won the doll for me at Asbury Park one summer when he was on furlough from the Army fighting the Germans.

When Butch, my black, shaggy dog, bit my cousin Ronnie, my mother said, "We can't keep Butch with us anymore." She gave him to my Aunt Lisa, who had no children then. I could still see him when we visited, but it was not the same. Over the more than sixty years since these tales, many people I loved left my life, either by death or through disagreement. I even have a younger sister who doesn't speak to me, because I cannot meet her expectations of me. I do and have mourned all of these losses and miss the folks I no longer have by my side, including my sister, my parents, my grandparents

51

and Aunt Lisa, who took Butch and who advised me to marry Bob. She died this year at the age of ninety-eight.

But to lose someone to Alzheimer's disease, as I have now done for the second time in my life is the worst loss of all because they are still with you. They look the same; they smile, but not the same way. The sparkle that was there just for me is gone.

It seems like all of a sudden to me now, but it must have been building up for a while. My husband first stops doing most of what he had always done. He spends his time sleeping or reading or watching Mr. Bean videos on his VHS machine in his room. He becomes angry with me and paranoid, accusing me of sexual adventures outside the marriage. He accuses me of wanting him to die, so I could get his money. He is loud. This quiet, peaceful, loving man changes into this bullying, angry person without provocation. He also accuses me of always wanting to be the boss, making all the decisions (he's right on that score; I wish it were not the case).

No matter what I say, I can't get through to him. So I learn an invaluable lesson. I cannot do this alone. I cannot fix this. I cannot control it. I need help and education and I need to learn to be considerate of the feelings of my husband. Just because he has no more short term memory, just because he doesn't know one day from the next, or when my birthday is, or our anniversary, just because he can no longer locate anything in our 1100 square foot apartment doesn't mean I can ignore him, put up with his volatile behavior, care for his physical needs and go on with our lives.

7 – Sexual Misbehavior

New York, March 2008

"You better watch out," Bob says to Corina, our housekeeper, as I pay her for the day's work. Corina smiles. She's expecting to hear a funny story from my husband.

"You're the same size as my wife," he continues, "If your back is turned, I may come after you one day instead of her." Now Bob is smiling and I am ready to crawl under the floorboards. Corina says a quick good-bye and exits.

The Alzheimer's Association website has a list of behaviors associated with this disease and lists many suggestions for caregivers on behavior management. Sexualized behaviors are noted under Bold Behaviors. The website states, "Persons with Alzheimer's disease may forget they are married and make inappropriate comments or suggestions to others. It is wise for the caregiver not to make fun of the person, but to distract the person and suggest other activities in which to engage."

A few days later I get a call from Corina.

"Señora, I think it would be better to find someone else to clean your house. I don't think it is good for me to be there if you are in your office."

I had phoned the Alzheimer's Association Help line in January when Bob was ranting. Now they call me and ask if my husband would be interested in participating in a memory workshop for people with Early Stage Alzheimer's disease. I think it would be a fine idea, so I accept without discussing it with Bob. They schedule an interview for him on March 19 to see if he would be appropriate for the group. We overcome the first problem which is arriving at Lexington Avenue and 40th Street during rush hour. Bob is not happy to find himself among the rushing, crowding folks. At the Association office, we wait and Bob reads brochures for all the services offered by the association. He is quiet. One young woman, Lauren, greets us and ushers us into a room where Paulette, the more senior social worker is waiting. Both will interview Bob with me in the room, but only Lauren runs the group.

"This is my lucky day. I have three beautiful women to choose from. That Spitzer guy had to go all the way to Washington, D.C. and I have all three of you here in one room." This is how Bob starts the interview, as we sit in a circle of chairs. He is referring to the former governor of New York State who resigned recently due to the publicity over his patronage of escort services. Bob has been reading obsessively about the story. Paulette labels Bob's behavior,

"Bob, you are quite agitated this morning." I had understood the word "agitated" to relate only to the rage Bob had exhibited in January and I had only been giving him the 0.5 mg of Haldol when I saw that kind of rage. Paulette says he needs the medication daily. The social workers do not accept my husband for the group. They feel he would be disruptive to the others. In April, at our second Geriatric Clinic visit, Dr. B. concurs and we begin daily doses of the medication. But before the medication takes effect, we have dinner with Bob's nephew Stewart and his wife Irene, who are in the city from Florida for the optician's show. We are joined for dinner by Bob's niece, Jeannie and her boyfriend, Gary.

"Aunt Phyllis," Jeannie whispers, "before the evening is over, can I talk to you privately for a few minutes?"

After dinner, we sit over a cup of coffee and I listen.

"You must have noticed," Jeannie begins, "I haven't been around much lately."

"True," I respond.

I have been pretty preoccupied lately. Jeannie and Gary were very helpful on moving day last year when we relocated to the new apartment. They kept Bob focused so I could manage the movers. She also helped me restock the refrigerator and empty the boxes of food. Gary is a stamp salesman, so he and Bob discuss stamp collection and sales matters. Bob would like to sell his remaining collection, but the price has to be right. Gary is planning an auction. We have had some contact, but less now than before.

Jeannie continues, "Uncle Bobby called me up one day and invited me to lunch, and he said I wouldn't even have to sleep with him for him to pay for lunch." Jeannie waits for me to react before she continues, "And one day when I was at your apartment, he put his hand all the way up my thigh. I didn't say anything, but I stayed away. He's never acted this way before. I can't even look at him."

I empathize with her creeped-out feelings, and explain that Bob has lost his inhibition. Whatever comes into his mind, he says. I explained that this symptom is part of his illness and that hyper-sexuality has been a concern of his (and mine) for a while. Hopefully, the new medication will reduce or eliminate it.

We will never know if the medication or time itself changed Bob's sexualized focus, but it did moderate, towards me and towards others. He still, however, keeps up a monologue, cataloguing women we see in the street, or on the subway, by the size of their breasts or butts, but I pretend not to hear him. This behavior continues throughout the summer, when there is a lot of exposed skin to observe.

When we move to Arizona for the winter, Bob is distracted by his garage workshop. He makes replicas of a jewelry box he had made many years ago. During the winter he completes seven boxes, with drawers and knobs. Each is done less skillfully than the one before and none matches the original in finish or precision. It seems as though Bob is unaware of the quality of the work. He focuses on the completion of each project, often staying up late to work in the garage.

Bob is not distracted from his hyper-sexualized interest in me, though. Our new house adds to my sense of exposure because the master bath is connected to the master bedroom by an arch. There's no door except for the one to a separate toilet room. And you can see through the arch to the mirrored wall above the double sinks, which looks great. But you can also see into the glass- walled shower. Bob wants to watch me take a shower.

"I'll just pull up a chair and sit here. You don't have to do a thing," he wheedles.

How our lives are changed. We looked forward to taking showers together in this new house; we've always enjoyed the intimacy of the experience. Now he only wants to watch. He wants to watch me dress and undress, too, and I feel as if I exist only for his visual pleasure. Teasing doesn't work. The only solution I find is to dress and undress in the walk-in closet, and to shower in the guest bathroom. What he doesn't see, he doesn't ask for.

The next problem occurs in bed. As Bob is staying awake longer at night, he sleeps more in the daytime. His circadian rhythm is off. He awakens with an erection at all hours of the night and wants to have sex. At first I am drowsy and I oblige him, since he cannot achieve penetration and soon falls back asleep. But to be deprived of sleep every night wears on me and I can no longer tolerate it. I am crabby during the daytime. I have no energy. If I refuse there will be outrage. I certainly cannot tolerate rage behavior in the early hours before dawn.

Finally, I have no choice. I move to the guest bedroom. He does not follow me. He sulks for days. I understand why, but I haven't yet figured out how to deal with this problem. Eventually, I find the answer. I set a time.

"Bob, you can't roll over to my side of the bed unless it is seven a.m. or later."

This works for a while. Then he starts awakening me during the night again.

"I can't see the clock from here," is his next excuse.

I move the clock radio to his nightstand. This behavior disrupts my feelings toward my husband. I begin to see him as a teenager trying to score, rather than a loving sexual partner. The joy is gone, the partnership is gone. I feel like a servant.

8 – Good Adjustments

We return to Arizona for Mother's Day and Grant's fifth birthday. Linda is excited about new housing construction barely four miles from her house and from Steve's house as well. The homes will be sold at pre-boom prices. Bob sees the model homes and falls in love with one of them and says, "I can picture us living here in the winters" as he gazes from the large picture window. We decide to buy one.

Our house will have with 36 inch doorways, a handicap accessible bath and no steps, on a corner lot away from through streets. I will hire help as needed, but my husband will live out his days with as much freedom and dignity as possible. I am happy we will buy this house while Bob can still learn his way around it, be familiar with it and enjoy it, before those skills disappear. Since my mother was confined to a wheelchair at the end of her life; I figure Bob might be, too.

In July, the construction begins. Bob is so excited by the photos Steve sends, he wants to see for himself what the workers are doing, so we travel to Arizona for a two-week trip so Bob can approve the construction. The trip is so successful that I respond to the invitation from my cousin Nora in Switzerland, who has invited us to her birthday party in August.

Yes, we will come. It will be our last European vacation.

Nora and Robi meet us at the airport, transport us to our hotel and show us how to use the tram to travel around Zurich, which is not totally unfamiliar to us. We have visited before when Steve accompanied us to Europe. I am excited to spend time with my cousin. We travel with Nora and Robi by train to Arosa, a small ski town in the Alps, where we stay in a charming hotel and ride to the top of the mountain in an enclosed cabin ski lift and walk down, listening to cowbells chiming. Bob walks arm in arm with Nora, ecstatic. We even fly by ourselves to Prague, in the Czech Republic, where we spend four days sightseeing. Having so much activity with no responsibility for cooking or any household tasks has us both remembering past trips and seduces us into thinking everything is all right.

In November, we return to Arizona to a completed house. Bob is animated, speaking of the house constantly, waiting for it to be furnished so we can move in. He loves the twelve foot ceilings, which make the rooms look big. He loves the three car garage, one of which will be outfitted for a workshop for him. Mesa, Arizona is part of the Sonoran Desert, and as such is built on hard rock, making the construction of basements extremely expensive. Our house is built on a slab. It has a stone facade, a tiled roof and an arched entryway. All of the homes are painted stucco in sand and ochre colors, with pale peach and mocha tones for accent. Our home, on a corner lot sits alone for now on its barren, dusty street, filled with large yellow heavy machinery and the sound of hammers and saws.

When we move from Linda's house to our own, Bob misses Grant and Waldo, the cat. It feels kind of lonely. We have no neighbors yet, no landscaping and just enough furniture to eat and sleep, except for patio furniture so we can enjoy the wonderful, sunny weather. Steve has a great idea.

"Why don't you babysit for Pebbles? She's lonely too, when I'm at work," he suggests. Pebbles is his 5 year old half-blind dachshund. We agree and each morning during the week, Steve drops the dog off on his way to work and picks her up again in the evening. Steve praises Bob's accomplishments in the garage, listens to stories of his pooch's antics, and stays for dinner and chat, if he likes what's on the menu. The little dog becomes another joy of Bob's life. Bob feeds Pebbles small scraps of everything, much to Steve's chagrin, and delights when Pebbles eats what Bob thinks she will like. We take the dog for a walk to the mailbox each day, providing a bit more exercise for Bob, as he does a lot of walking in New York, but not here.

Steve also helps Bob establish his workshop. Together, they scour the town, looking for a wooden workbench the two of them can put together themselves. Steve also purchases three large boxes of old, rusty tools. They build the workbench, Bob purchases a grinder to attach to the workbench, and I pick up a stool, so he can sit while he works. Bob shines, polishes and sharpens all the tools. He is so happy. *So am I.*

Proud of the furnishings and the color scheme of the house, Bob overemphasizes its value when he speaks of it to his friends and relatives back east. He claims often that he "feels like a millionaire here." He also uses words like "luxurious" and "expansive" when he speaks of the house. His descriptive language makes it seems as if we're living in a mansion. It is of course twice the size of our New York apartment but maybe half the size of our old house. Bob has some initial difficulty finding his way around. He makes signs for himself and posts them on the doors 'laundry room', 'garage', 'bathroom', 'my office'. He still often enters the master bedroom when he is looking for the garage. Whenever a guest arrives, Bob offers to take the visitors on a tour of the house. My friend Marilynn hires a caregiver to stay with her demented spouse and comes for a few days of respite. My friend Adele escapes the New York winter for a week, and Irving, Bob's brother visits from Florida for another week. All of these visitors the first winter. Life is good.

Bob spends most of each day and night in the garage workshop. When we shipped our car to Arizona we packed the trunk full of wood scraps Bob found on the streets of New York. Bob sorts through all of his wood, trying to see if he has what he needs to make a jewelry box. We have brought with us a jewelry box with four drawers that Bob made many years ago. He wants to copy it now. Each step of the process is a challenge for him. First, the found wood isn't smooth enough. So we buy more. Then, his hand saw doesn't cut straight enough the first time. So he cuts a new piece. Then the new piece breaks. I feel frustrated for him, but I am so proud of his persistence. He is determined to make the jewelry box. He makes the four drawers first, and then the frame is not cut evenly enough, so the drawers don't fit. He makes the shelves. We go to the arts and crafts store, and purchase a wood plaque with beveled edges, which fits the frame Bob has constructed like a door. We buy a knob and hinges, and one box is complete! He stains and varnishes the finished project, but he hasn't the patience to sand the pieces very smoothly.

We use the four drawers as a template and we have Home Depot cut the wood for a second jewelry box, and finally the drawers fit. He is so proud of himself, but it doesn't look at all like the box he made earlier in his life. *Does he even notice?*

When Bob tires of jewelry boxes, I draw the dimensions for a computer wires box, which he makes for me. The walnut stained box sits on the floor behind my desk and keeps all the wires hidden and the modem and wireless router neatly in view. When Linda asks for one however, he doesn't make another.

Meanwhile, Bob's illness is progressing. Bob has problems again with task completion. He will forget to eat the food he has set out for himself. He forgets to put his dishes into the sink, or into the dishwasher. *These are all tasks he did automatically just a few weeks ago.* He also forgets where to find things in the new house, but that is understandable and Bob's attitude has been great. When it isn't, I think it is because he has forgotten to take his medications.

I know how Bob hates to be reminded. Even a kind reminder is experienced as a nag, so now I put the breakfast on the table, with his morning medications in sight before I leave for the gym. If I've learned anything, it's that I need to take care of myself if I want to be able to take care of Bob. The gym is not an indulgence; it's a requirement. When I return, I prepare another meal. I don't ask what he would like and I don't call it lunch. I call him in from the garage. "Food is on the table," I sometimes just say, or "It's time for a break." "In five minutes," he says, or "I have to wash my hands" and he comes in and eats.

We have a problem when Bob gets hungry later. He needs to eat immediately. So he prepares cheese, bread and tea, but then he is not hungry for supper. So now I prepare a pot of soup. If he gets hungry early, he eats a bowl of soup with some crackers and is still able to eat dinner at 6 or 6:30.

Bob's taste in food has changed. He won't eat fish anymore. As we haven't eaten beef in twenty years, we eat a lot of chicken. He said the other day, "You know I am a much better cook than you." *I know. I wish you would cook again. We're both bored with my cooking our limited diet.*

Tomorrow is Inauguration Day. Barack Obama is to be sworn in as president the day after Martin Luther King's birthday. And I have no one with whom to share this auspicious moment. I invite Grant to spend the night, but I wake up in a bad mood. Dave comes to pick Grant up, and as I try to apologize for sending the boy home, Dave puts his arm around me and gives me a hug! So surprising and welcome! I wanted to be by myself, so I tell Bob I'm going shopping. But he wants to come with me, so I keep my bad mood to myself. We watch a football game on Sunday afternoon at Linda's.

The Arizona Cardinals will go to the Super Bowl in two weeks. That's very important here.

One reason I am sad today stems from my conversation with my husband yesterday. Sometimes he is very able to communicate his feelings.

"I'm getting dumber and dumber every day," he began. "I'm having trouble understanding the words I read, and I'm too lazy to look them all up in the dictionary." It is so sad to see his awareness of his decline, but he doesn't give up.

I am so lonesome. I miss the man he was. I am so appreciative that I am not stuck in the dyad, just the two of us alone in a big city. I love having family around who can diffuse a situation if it gets tough, but my life with my husband will never be the same again.

Dave volunteers to landscape our back yard. Bob and I drive to the plant nursery with Dave and Grant, purchase trees and plants, including an orange tree and a grapefruit tree, which Dave plants for us. He is a good designer and knows proportion and size and shade quality of shrubs and trees. After the trees and bushes are planted, I watch Bob place stones around the base of each of the 27 plants and trees. He waters and fertilizes, weeds and trims. He's a happy gardener.

Grant sleeps over in "his" room, which he generously shares with our guests. One day, Dave has 23 tons of gravel delivered to the house. Bob and Grant rake it all from wheelbarrow-sized piles left all over the yard. Dave later spends two hours raking the whole yard, evening out the gravel. He is a perfectionist who appreciated the help of his "team".

Bob says, "Every day is vacation in Arizona." He comes with me to personally fill the gas tank and he checks the level in the car each time we leave the house. We go to the farmer's market so Bob can choose the best fruits and vegetables, but mostly he prefers to stay home and work in his garage workshop. Bob is sweet. He loves Pebbles and Steve and Grant, he tells me daily what a wonderful wife I am, he worries about my younger son Ted and thinks Linda is beautiful.

9 – Finding Meaningful Work

New York, spring 2009

I truly believe that members of The Great Generation need work experience to feel alive and useful. Those who are a bit older than my husband, revel in their war stories. Bob loves to tell Army stories and will, to anyone who will listen. He was a clerk, stationed in Japan after the Korean War, not a fighter. For the Baby Boomers, I think recreation gives their life meaning. When they retire and for many all their lives, a good tennis match or a golf outing, if no longer in person, then on television, works to make them feel as if they belong to a group of people who are interested in the same things, who are knowledgeable and can converse about the same players, scores, and techniques. For those of us in the eighth decade of our lives, creativity reigns supreme. We draw, paint, write, knit, quilt, and take pictures – enjoying the experience as we never could during our professional career days or while we were raising our families.

For Bob it has always been work, whether at his job or around the house. He does not relax. As a retiree, he worked at making travel plans, until he was no longer able to master the planning. He works still at reading, sitting with a dictionary, trying to relearn Chemistry 101. I think it is remarkable that he bought a chemistry book at a used book store and tries to understand it. He is unsuccessful which upsets him. If he is not working, he falls asleep.

Bob purchased jeans in Arizona this past winter, 2009, and brought them to New York to hem on his sewing machine. When he is calm, due to the new medicine, he tries to thread the sewing machine. He is busy in his room for some time, quietly.

Then he comes to find me, "I can't do it," he says.

"Do what?" I ask.

"I can't get this thing to work," he answers.

"What seems to be the problem?" I want to know specifics, if possible. Maybe there is something I can help with. "I can't make the thread work," he responds.

"Come with me," I say. We go to the computer. The Singer Sewing Machine Company has a website that has a specific video on how to thread a sewing machine. Bob studies the video and goes back into his room. The lesson is successful, but the heavy seam on the jeans material breaks the needle. Bob travels by subway by himself, to 27th Street, where there are sewing machine repair stores. When he asks the price for a needle he tells the clerk they are too expensive and returns home. Without my knowledge, Bob then takes the pants to the tailors and has them altered. He keeps the receipt and remembers to pick the pants up at the cleaners. I see the completed project.

"What's up? Did you have these hemmed?" I ask.

"Yes, I am not sewing anymore. It's just not worth it. It's too hard for me to do." Bob is calm, but sad.

Bob no longer feels competent at the sewing machine, because he has no need to use the machine often. He no longer wears dress shirts. The ones he owns he has previously sewn to the correct sleeve length. He has many pair of khakis and jeans and he refuses my friend Adele's request to sew aprons for her grandchildren. I purchase stained glass kits and jig saw puzzles but Bob doesn't enjoy craft projects outside the woodworking workshop. He does not play cards anymore or cook. He will fix the salad, if I set out all the ingredients, the bowl and the knife. No, he will choose his own knife. The one I lay out is never the right one.

Bob has completed the book sorting. There is no need to go to the storage facility any longer. Making the bed and folding the clean laundry are not enough to stimulate him for the day.

He walks to Gristede's, the grocery store two blocks away where he buys milk and ice cream. He also enjoys walking to Zabar's, the gourmet food store where he purchases good freshly baked bread and olives. To get to Zabar's he walks to Broadway, two long avenue blocks and then down six blocks to 80th Street. He has narrowed his safe zone in the neighborhood to about fourteen blocks north and six blocks south, and three blocks east from Broadway to Columbus.

I plan outings for us for every day I do not have office hours. We travel to the places on our "New York City Walks – 50 Adventures to Do on Foot" cards. Our friends Sandy and Herbie gave us this deck of cards as a housewarming gift.

We visit Arthur Avenue, an Old Italian shopping and dining district in the Bronx, the Brooklyn Botanical Gardens, and the Lower East Side where Chinese, Italian and Jewish immigrants each settled when they first arrived in the United States. When grandson Austin arrives for a visit, we travel by subway to Fort Tryon Park and the Cloisters with its magnificent medieval sculptures, artifacts and paintings. We lunch on the boardwalk in Brighton Beach where the Russian immigrant population has settled.

Planning these excursions works for a while to keep my husband alert and interested in life. Bob travels by himself by train on Jersey Transit to Dover, New Jersey every other week to visit his best friend, Eliot. This works out well on days while I'm at the office.

One evening in April, 2009, Bob does not return to New York on time. I try to call him on his cell phone but he doesn't answer. Eliot confirms he saw Bob board the 5:04 train at Dover. We both worry. At 8:40, Bob phones. He is at the local CVS pharmacy and wants to pick up a prescription; he has been told that I have already been there. What should he do?

"Come on home, dear." Gee, it is so hard to be calm and proactive. *Where were you? Don't you realize how worried we were?* Of course I wanted to shake him. What happened?

Eventually I find out that he was disoriented in Penn Station. He found a police officer and asked to be directed to the subway. Neither Bob nor the officer indicated *which* subway. Bob was directed to the Eighth Avenue ACE lines. He doesn't recognize them. Needing the Uptown 1 train, Bob finally boards an Uptown 2 express train, which doesn't stop on 86th St. He disembarks at 96th St. and, fearful of making another error, walks the ten blocks home, passing the CVS on the way, and remembering he had dropped off a prescription the day before.

Getting disoriented in Penn Station can happen to anyone. But Bob is shaken by the experience and will no longer travel to New Jersey on the train. He also begins to be uncomfortable alone in the apartment during my work hours. I am now only seeing patients two days each week. Bob meets me for dinner each evening at our local diner. After dinner, I return to the office, and he returns home. One evening, he fails to show up for dinner. Frantic, I walk home; he's not there and he doesn't answer his cell phone. Bob was calmly waiting at another diner, but claims it was too noisy to hear the phone ringing.

I had been in contact with an agency that sends volunteers to visit homebound adults. Dorot, the agency, sends a really sweet man one hour each week, during my office hours. I change my schedule so I'm home for dinner, ordering in or picking up something for us to eat on my way. I cannot survive this way. I have no life. I'm either seeing patients, or catering to my husband. I'm tired all the time.

10 – And Still More Diagnoses

Arizona, spring 2009

More than two years have passed since the diagnosis – years in which I traveled through denial, through anger, through depression – I am tired of fighting with my own anger at the disease. I understand my inability to control or cure my husband's illness; I deal with my depression by talking with others, by exercising and by writing. By now, I should come to acceptance, right? Not yet, I am still at the bargaining stage, still hoping for a different diagnosis, one that could be treated. At least I wish I could find a prescription for medication that would keep my husband mentally alive.

My family in Arizona and I are all getting used to the idea that Bob is slowing down. We are happy that the medication, 0.5 mg Haldol, is helping him remain the sweet, loving guy I married. The Namenda medication is helping Bob do his projects in the garage; he is not depressed.

"If you need me, I'll be in the garage. There's something I'm doing out there," he says.

Bob loves shopping for new tools and sharpening or polishing the ones he already owns. Just looking at them, neatly arrayed in his new cabinets, makes him happy. Anticipating a visit from his brother, Irving, he sharpens his tools. The new grinder Bob purchases is possibly to impress his brother. Irving was a career machinist for the city of New York. I do know that Bob smiles happily when his brother praises the workman-ship on the old, rusty tools Bob cleaned and sharpened.

Things are working out so well I can see we will spend our winters from now on in Arizona. I decide to find an internist. For one thing I need someone to pre-scribe refills for Bob's medications. For another we need a doctor who knows us. I recall how difficult it was in New York to get help when we needed it. My son Steve recommends Dr. R., whom he has consulted for fifteen years. I make an appointment. The doctor's office is located in a strip mall on Power Road, not ten minutes from our house. A Tae Kwan Do shop is next door. We park right in front of the entrance. The doctor is a solo practitioner, with a receptionist and a nurse in charge of the modest office: a long, narrow waiting room, chairs with black leather seats on chrome bases lining the walls. Prints of Arizona landscapes adorn the walls at predictable intervals. A water cooler is the room's main attraction.

Both young women are friendly and welcoming. We sit in the leather chairs and are handed the requisite clip board with pages of forms. I reluctantly fill out the forms. It feels so infantilizing to answer the questions for him. But the alternative is having Bob ask me the answer to every question. I think that makes him feel worse. Actually this is the most comprehensive set of history information ever required of us.

Bob says as he watches me write, "I don't know our Arizona address or telephone number."

That's understandable. We have only been here a short while. That he doesn't remember our New York address is another matter. Dr. R. greets us at his office door. He is not a tall man. He has a captivating smile with bright white teeth shining from his round face. His black hair is a bit long and straight. He introduces himself, directs Bob to sit up on the exam table, and props himself next to Bob to sit and read the forms I have filled out! *I am quietly impressed.*

He tells us, "I am so happy you have come, to be new patients, after most of the other winter visitors have left. In the winter, I wouldn't have had enough time to devote to you." After he finishes reading, he begins to examine my husband's eyes, nose and throat while asking Bob questions.

This is a great method for engaging Bob in the process. He is being touched, which grounds him. He is being looked at, so he can hear and concentrate. *I love this doctor already.*

After an hour of reading and examining, Dr. R. who is still sitting on the side of the exam table, next to my husband, places his hand on Bob's arm and begins to talk.

"I am not so sure your cognitive decline is entirely due to Alzheimer's disease. There might be other reasons for memory loss, which could be fixed. Let's explore one of those. "*I am all ears.*

Dr. R. continues, "I see by history and by exam that you snore loudly. Is this true?" He is looking at Bob.

"I don't know." Bob shrugs, "I just sleep."

"I think," continues the physician, "you may have something called Sleep Apnea. This could cause a lack of oxygen in the brain which effects memory. I think your case merits a visit to a sleep disorders clinic to ascertain if this is the case."

Since it is nearly time for us to return to New York, I thank Dr. R. profusely and tell him we will pursue this in the city. When we return to New York, I tell this story to my friend Sandy, a retired nursing administrator who now works as a supervisor of student nursing. Sandy tells me that she has just returned from a 50th reunion of her nursing school graduation class, where she spent some time with Dr. W., another class member and currently the director of a sleep disorders clinic associated with New York University Medical Center. *A happy coincidence.*

I schedule an appointment and we arrive by bus at the 25th St and Fifth Avenue office. We enter a spartan room, light wood paneled, with a long, narrow corridor separating the waiting room/reception area from the doctors' offices. We are the only ones in the waiting area. A receptionist guides us to Dr. B.'s office. He introduces himself and explains the concept of sleep disorders. He is lecturing. Bob appears to be listening, but I don't know how much he comprehends as he asks no questions of the doctor. Dr. B. then invites Dr. W. to join us. She has read the medical history I have provided. The two doctors agree that a sleep disorders test is indicated.

We are shown the rest of the suite. There is a sleep room with a bathroom. It looks like a budget motel room with a single bed, except the television is a computer monitor that can be viewed from outside the room. They show us the computer that will measure respiration, snoring, REM sleep and the other stages of sleep. They show Bob the finger cot that he will wear so that his heart rate will be measured as well. They show him the several contacts that will be placed on his head.

Bob starts, "It looks like you're going to be experimenting on my brain."

The doctor smiles, "I guess you could say that."

"If you're going to experiment on me and get data recorded about my brain, I want to get paid to be a part of your experiment." Bob states clearly. He was listening, but not exactly understanding.

"How much are we talking?" quips Dr. B.

"How much do you charge for the visit?" asks Bob.

"I'll give you one per cent," teases the doctor.

Bob laughs and we walk out to the front office to schedule the sleepover. On the way to the bus stop, Bob says, "Phyllis, I'm not letting anyone experiment on my brain. If you think I'm going back there, you're nuts." He is adamant.

I phone to cancel the sleep study and speak, apologizing, to Dr. W.

"Not to worry," she says, "I understand. I've been there." As I am about to hang up, she adds, "By the way, I noticed as your husband was walking up the hall with Dr. B. that one shoulder hangs lower than the other and that his gait is uneven. Also he jests and jokes, but his affect is flat. Have you noticed these things?"

"No, actually I haven't. But I have noticed that he is tripping on small cracks in the sidewalk." I tell her he has fallen twice. I'm afraid for him to walk alone in the street.

"That's another reason to see a neurologist," she says. I have a colleague at NYU, Dr. H. He's on the faculty at the medical school and he is an expert in Parkinson's disease. I think you should consult with him."

So in May, we have the aborted sleep disorders visit and in June we meet with Dr. H. at NYU. He examines Bob, asks to see the original MRI, and as it is two years since the first MRI, orders a new one. He discontinues the 0.5 mg Haldol and replaces it with 25 mg Xanax, three times daily, for agitation. He doesn't like the Prozac Bob has been taking for 20 years, and slowly weans him from it, substituting 100 mg of Zoloft, the generic name being Sertraline. He tests Bob's reflexes as he asks Bob questions.

"Let's go for a walk," he says and he watches Bob walk up and down the hospital corridor. After a mini-mental exam and a Parkinson behavior study, he diagnoses Bob with early Parkinson's disease. Dr. H. explains that cognitive decline is usually seen later in the progression of the illness, but that sometimes, as in Bob's case, it can start earlier. The Sinemet medication can control it, and slow down further deterioration. He agrees that Bob's limbs are rigid, his facial expressions blank. Dr. H. starts Bob on Sinemet, building it up over time from one to three times daily. He also describes the increased memory retention possibility of an Exelon patch which he has tried with patients who were also taking Namenda and gives us a trial sample, but tells me to try it for one day only. "If it works, it works fast," he says. If we see no immediate dramatic change, forget about it. I try it for the one day, but see no appreciable difference in Bob's memory and discontinue it.

In July, Bob falls out of bed, perhaps hitting his head on the corner of the dresser or the closet door. I am wakened by the sound of his fall.

"Bob, are you ok?" I turn on the light. Bob is curled up on the floor between the bed and the closet door, which is not quite closed. *I am frightened.* He is drowsy, but conscious. I let him remain there until he tries to get up, then help him back into bed.

"I want to sleep," he says.

I know from rearing three children that sleep is not what you want the patient to do if you suspect a concussion. But it is 5:30 in the morning and I don't want to call an ambulance. I fear that would be frightening for him and make the situation worse. So I watch and I wait. Suddenly I recall that our insurance company, Blue Cross and Blue Shield, has a telephone service. I call, a nurse answers and after listening to what happened, we agree to let Bob sleep, but to wake him every two hours to see if he rouses, focuses his eyes, drinks some water.

"If in six hours, he is not recovered, go to the emergency room," the nurse advises. She phones two hours later to check on Bob's condition. She advises me to let him sleep for another two hours. I wait two more hours. I check on my sleeping husband. *Should I wake him to take his medications? Should I let him rest?* As it is now 9:30, I phone Dr. A.'s office, literally on the same block as our apartment. The nurse practitioner listens, but refuses to comment as she has not seen the patient. She does not want me to bring Bob to the office.

"If you go to the emergency room, go to Lenox Hill Hospital. That's where Dr. A. is affiliated," she advises.

I phone Dr. H. He's new to Bob's case, but he does talk to me personally and listens to the whole story.

"If you do go to the ER," Dr. H. advises, "Ask them not to admit him, just to do a CAT scan as an outpatient."

Bob sleeps on and off all day while I struggle to make the right decision. The weekend is coming up and there might not be anyone available to read the results of the CAT scan, if Bob gets one done the following day. I need a professional evaluation of Bob's condition. It's four in the afternoon when I decide to take Bob to the ER — just for a CAT scan. I help Bob dress and we take a taxi to the hospital. Of course, they take one look at him, place him in a wheelchair and admit him. We are in the ER for hours. Bob has a heparin lock placed 'just in case' there is a need to administer medication intravenously. They do a chest X-ray, draw blood and perform the CAT scan. Bob is wheeled on the gurney to all parts of the hospital for the various tests. There is a long wait between transfers.

Now there's a wait for someone to read the X-ray and the CAT scan. It is Friday evening. I can see that Bob is improving. He is hungry. "Get this tube out of my arm," he says to me, annoyed. He wants to sit up. The staff is very understanding. They bring him Jell-O, but they say it is hospital policy not to remove the tubes or let him be up or dressed until he is released by the Emergency Room doctor. Eventually, we are cleared to go. Bob, they say, has a concussion. He will be dizzy for a few days. The CAT scan also reveals that Bob has had a stroke or a series of mild strokes, but not recently. That's scary as well. They give me lists of possible symptoms, and when to return to the ER if needed. I request copies of the results of all of the tests to take with me.

Bob walks to the exit as I want to make sure he is steady on his feet as we leave the hospital.

"Wait right here," I tell him when we walk outside. "I'll go to the curb to hail a cab." My husband responds true to form.

"What do we need a cab for? There's a subway right here on the corner. Why are you wasting my money on cabs all day?"

I remember he has had no medication all day. *The subway goes downtown and we live cross-town, I want to remind him.* I am tired, hungry and cranky. I stay quiet, knowing I can only make matters worse. I hail a cab. I put one foot in the cab, looking at Bob, who is watching me, glowering. He follows me into the cab and we go home.

As I reflect on the day, I am once again grateful to Dr. R., who set me on this track toward finding a new diagnosis. Bob's tripping and falling, although they had made me anxious about Bob traveling about the city on his own, had never been acknowledged by me as symptoms of a disease other than one caused by memory failure. I also appreciate Dr. H, who speaks with me personally when needed, is not an alarmist and is willing to give me practical advice. He also communicated with our internist and promised to work together with him. I feel I am building a team who will help me care for my husband.

11 – A Good Combination

Last year, at the time of the Jewish New Year, Bob assured me that he would attend services with me in the morning, which he did. This year, when the morning comes, he wants to stay in bed. I show him his suit, shirt and tie that we chose last evening for him to wear.

"All right, I'll go. But just this once. Don't make me go again." He showers, dresses, eats breakfast and we leave. He greets our friends; he is happy to see everyone. During the service, he leafs through the prayer book and falls asleep during the sermon. I understand that he is unable to follow the service any longer. Afterwards, we return home, eat a light lunch and I remind him not to change out of his suit and tie, as we are traveling by train to his son's home in New Jersey. This is the first year we do not own a car in the city; we shipped it to Arizona during the summer.

Last year we drove to New Jersey to visit his family.

"I don't remember agreeing to do this," Bob says. "It's a long ride. What is so important about going there for dinner? We have food here." Bob is whining like a school kid, not wanting to go to school.

"You'll have fun," I say. "We'll take the subway to Penn Station, we'll get on the train and you'll be able to see from the window all of New Jersey go by." I respond as to a child, which I don't like doing, but I want Bob to look forward to the visit.

"I want to read the paper," Bob says petulantly.

"Let's take the paper with us. There will be plenty of time to read it on the train." I have an answer for every objection.

"My fingers will get all dirty," says Bob. He's got a response for everything, too.

"There's a bathroom on the train. You can wash them before we get to Adam's station," I continue.

"Just a few more minutes," he stalls.

"Okay, but we have to leave here by 2, as the train leaves Penn Station at 2:45 and we don't want to miss it. Adam will be waiting at the station when we get there, and they will hold dinner until we get back. It will take a half hour to get to Adam's house from the train station." *Enough already. I can play this game with a straight face and no attitude for just so long.*

"All right, let's go. I just have to get my things." Bob walks into his room.

"Where is my wallet?" Bob is in the hallway, asking me. "I need those pieces of paper for my pocket."

"There are Kleenex boxes in each bathroom and the kitchen." I say. I understand the word he is looking for but I am getting frustrated.

"Be with you in a minute. I just have to make a contribution first." He enters the bathroom. Pretty soon we are on our way. We have no difficulties at the station. The train however is delayed and we have to wait.

"How will Adam know the train is late?" Bob wants to know.

"Let's call him and tell him," I answer.

"It's too noisy here. I can't hear myself think. Where are all these people going?" Bob gets sidetracked. I phone Adam. We board the train, find two seats next to a large window and settle in for the hour and a half ride. Bob's fine. I read my book; Bob reads his newspaper, interrupting my reading to tell me something interesting he finds, which is great. Before this summer and the new medications, he was not telling me anything about what he read in the paper. I pick up one section of the paper with which he is finished. The written story does not match what he has told me. *Okay. He is reading, but making up his own stories.*

We arrive at the station and Bob does not immediately see his son. Bob is anxious, looking for him. Adam is in the car, parked facing away from the station. He sees us and waves.

"Where were you? Didn't we call you and tell you we would be late? Did you just get here?" Adam touches his father on the shoulder, listening to his anxious comments.

"Hi, Dad. Let's go. I'm here, not to worry." Adam sounds good. We get into the car; Bob sits in front with his son. There is no more conversation until we get to their home. Sheree, Adam's wife, greets us warmly, and their daughters, Jessica and Gabrielle shyly say hello. They are not comfortable with their changed grandfather or with themselves. They are 12 and 11 now, no longer little girls who play hide and seek with Pop-Pop. The poodle, Cane, greets us by peeing on the floor. Sheree goes to wipe up and we enter the house.

"This is such a big house," Bob exudes, "You've done a great job outside. The grass, the plants..."

We are the last of the guests to arrive and dinner is waiting. We are ushered into the dining room, introduced to the two families who are regularly invited to these holiday dinners with their children. The girls help serve the meal for the first time this year. They are careful and gracious. None of the adults converse with us. It is too far to the other end of the table. Really, the conversation is mostly between each parent and their children, about the food.

Bob gets up from the table between courses and begins to play with the dog. I sit quietly, watching as the two of them frolic in the front hall, next to the dining room. When dinner is completed, the children disappear to their playroom on the lower level of the house, the women help with the dishes and the three men converse at their end of the table. Bob and I sit.

I ask, "Adam, how about getting out the family picture albums and looking at them with your Dad?" Adam takes my suggestion, gets the albums. The two men have a good time identifying relatives in the pictures. There are many whom Bob does not recall. I help serve dessert and coffee. The children are called for dessert.

As Bob sees the skies darkening, he begins to worry. "How are we getting home?" he asks.

"We have hired a car and driver to drive you back to the city," Sheree says.

"When will he get here? It is getting dark. How do we know he is a safe driver? How does he know where to go?" Bob is noticeably anxious.

"This is a man we have known for a while. He's a safe driver. We've asked him to be here at 7:45. This way you'll be home by 9 o'clock," Sheree answers calmly. She packs up leftovers for everyone and sends us home with the driver.

I ask Bob to sit in the back seat, thinking he will fall asleep. I sit up front with the driver. We talk about his SUV and his holiday celebrations and then I ask him about his business. "Oh, this driving is a sideline. During the regular week, I'm a pharmaceutical rep."

"Really? Do you know Adam was a pharmaceutical representative before he went to law school?" I add.

"I'm planning to go to medical school. That's why I'm driving, to save up money. We have this plan." The driver tells of his recent marriage.

"What area of pharmaceuticals do you represent?" I ask. I'm being polite. I don't want to know his life history.

"Elder care. My territory is Long Island," he says.

"What a coincidence! Do you know about medications for Alzheimer's disease?"

"Sure. I work with them every day," he boasts.

"How about..." I go through all the medications Bob has ever been prescribed, getting his feedback. When I get to the Exelon patch that Dr. H. had given me to try to see if it improved his memory, he says, "The nursing home staffs really like the delivery option of those."

"What about their efficacy?" I want to know.

"They work really well, as an add-on with Namenda, improving on-task performance and memory retention." says the driver.

Wow, I have a sample box of Exelon patches.

"Bob takes Namenda. I tried the Exelon patch for one day, but I didn't see any immediate result and I gave up," I say.

"You should give it a longer trial, since your husband takes Namenda already. You might see some good results," he suggests.

When we return home, I decide to try the Exelon patch. We have an appointment with Dr. H. in one week. Let's see. Bob agrees to try the patch. It is a round patch, smaller than a quarter in diameter, which is placed on the upper arm, changed daily, interchanging arms. This time I see a dramatic difference.

"Why do I have all these books about World War II?" Bob seeks out books from his own library and begins to reread them. He's curious. He finds an article about the destruction of the World Trade Center. He had forgotten about it. He is sad all over again. "People jumped out of the buildings," he says.

Bob starts paying attention to the news. "I'm not going to get any more shots," he says. "I take too many pills already. Do you think we'll get that swine flu?" he remembers. Bob asks Dr. H. about swine flu at our next appointment.

Choosing a movie to see, "Julie and Julia", Bob stays awake throughout it and later talks about Julia Child. He has read her cookbook and has watched her TV shows. The neurologist is surprised at this new talkative person he sees in his office. He attributes the change to the build-up of Sinemet in Bob's system. I don't know. Neither does the doctor. Whatever, it appears to be working. He writes a prescription for the Exelon patch and Bob and I are off for another six months in Arizona. We will be there from October until April this time, when Bob's family has planned a big family celebration.

12 – Freedom from Want

New York, fall 2009

I believe that we all retain bad feelings from conflicts that have not been resolved in childhood and that we revert to behaviors we used then to salve our bruised sense of ourselves when we are sick, injured or disabled. For example, people who were pampered as children are more apt to accept being cared for as adults. Those who fought against parental authority are likely to struggle against anything that looks like control by a caregiver.

You may think you know someone after you've been married, say, for thirty or forty years. I think I know some things about my husband after the mere twenty years we have been together. I know his stories – what formed him into the man I fell in love with – and I have some idea what lies behind the troublesome behaviors I begin to see now.

Bob was born in July, 1929, three months before the stock market crash. He was the second son following his brother, Irving, by seven years and the still birth of a baby girl three years before his birth. Irving says that his younger brother was coddled. Bob has often spoken about feeling imprisoned by an overprotective mother and by poverty. He complains, for example, that although his father was reputed to have played the violin, he wouldn't provide lessons for his son, "even though the young upstairs tenant would have given me lessons

for a quarter... I never heard my father play, but someone – one of Irving's children, I believe, still has my father's violin," he says.

When Bob tells the story it is clear that he still feels
a sense of deprivation. Similarly, he recalls having been
given a football which became deflated (through no
fault of his) shortly after its purchase, and was never
replaced. It's interesting that Irving recalls the same
incident, but *he* sees the football's purchase as the reason he did not get a record player that he very much
wanted. Clearly, the football incident is significant to
both brothers.

Bob's mother kept her son close for many reasons.
First, her baby was smaller in size than others. She
feared he would fail to thrive or be stunted in growth as
an adult. She provided HGH (human growth hormone)
shots when he was probably 10 or 11, "but the shots
hurt my arm, I wanted to play stickball on the street, so
I ran out of the doctor's office and refused to return,"
Bob explains when he tells this story. He grew to be
5'4", short for a guy, puberty was delayed to late ado-
lescence, but Bob is totally well proportioned.

Second, when Bob was five, he suffered a ruptured
appendix. Many years ago, when I first noticed what
looks like a puncture scar on his abdomen, Bob told
me, "One night, it must have been in 1934, I woke up in
pain. They rushed me to the hospital, where the doctors
performed an emergency appendectomy. I remember
lying on a bed with a tube connected to my arm, attached to a black box. I remember seeing a man, lying
on the adjacent bed, with a tube connected to his arm,

also attached to the same black box. I think now it was a blood transfusion. The next thing I remember is being in a crib. My Aunt Anna came to visit me and she brought a box of chocolate lollypops. The nurse took the box from my aunt, gave me one and handed out the rest to the other children in other cribs in the room. That wasn't fair. I remember feeling awful about that. No one asked me if I wanted to share my lollypops."

"They didn't let me go home to Brooklyn with my parents," he went on. "It was during the depression. I remember no one had jobs. They wanted me to have fresh fruit and vegetables, and sunshine to play in. They sent me to live with a foster family on a farm on Long Island. That must have been a social services agency that made the arrangements. The woman came to visit me at the farm, probably a social worker, and I said they weren't taking good care of me; they wouldn't let me go outside to play. She saw that my bandages were soiled, so I was moved to another foster care family, also on Long Island, a potato farm. Those people were nice to me and I got stronger. The social worker came and got me and brought me home."

"I was now six years old. My mother walked me down to the school. She told me to keep my hands folded on the desk and not to speak unless spoken to, as she watched through the glass in the door of the classroom. I had to go in myself. The other children were all seated at desks and I started first grade." He had missed the whole year of kindergarten. Now his mother had more reason to protect him. She didn't want her son taken from her.

Bob's interest in food preparation stems from that early time. His mother insisted that he eat to stay strong and to grow, but he didn't like his mother's cooking. Neither did Irving. To this day Irving won't eat chicken. He shudders at the memory of their mother's rubbery boiled chicken, served in the soup every Friday night. On Sundays Bob would be invited to dinner at the neighborhood homes of his friends, most of whom were Italian. Their kitchens smelled warm and inviting. Bob thought the food was delicious. His mother approved, as there he would eat heartily.

"They gave all the boys a little homemade wine with dinner," Bob recalled, "but not the girls." He started borrowing cookbooks from the library, and he began to cook when he was fourteen.

"I made a stuffed veal roast when my mother wasn't home and my father loved it," he recalls. "But my mother never made it or let me make it again." A love of food – good food – remains. Bob remembers the first taste he had of each different dish and where he was introduced to it. He told me about the first time he had a crown roast and the lamb chops had little paper feet on the ends. He recalled the mint jelly served with a leg of lamb. There have been so many of these stories throughout our years together, I never really understood their importance in his life. Bob has very exquisite taste buds and his sense of smell is very keen. He had read about these dishes and relished tasting them for the first time. I am sorry I didn't write the food stories down. Now they are all lost. After Irving left for his Army service in 1943, Bob's parents invited his father's brother, Uncle Harry, to stay with them as he had recently been divorced, thus adding a new influence to Bob's life.

"Uncle Harry bought me the most important gift I ever received, a one dollar chemistry set. My father made a space in the cellar for me to experiment." And so began Bob's lifelong interest in chemistry. Bob's father did not encourage his sons to go to college. Irving attended college for two years before being drafted. Because of his own difficulties during the depression, their father believed each son needed to learn a trade in order to earn a living. But Bob excelled in school. He was encouraged by a teacher to apply to Stuyvesant High School, one of three highly rated science high schools in the city, and he was accepted. There was little question then, that Bob would continue on to college. Along with the academic courses at Stuyvesant, Bob loved metal shop. "We were asked to bring in a quarter, which we melted down to make a ring. I couldn't afford a quarter, so the teacher melted down a nickel for my ring." Bob also loved woodshop, which is also still a major interest of his. Drafting was another matter. "My teacher said he had never seen a worse student in drafting," Bob told me. But later on, Bob designed and drew the plans for his own house. He must've learned how in that class.

Bob entered City College, where he majored in chemistry (remember the set he got from Uncle Harry?), but loved the German language classes and the music appreciation course. He knew every aria of the opera *Don Juan* by Mozart; could sing them all and could recognize the music whenever he heard it on the radio. Mozart has been his favorite composer since then.

Bob continued his studies for the PhD at Florida State University, in Tallahassee. During this time, however, Bob met Helen. When she left Florida to return to New York, Bob followed without completing his coursework and was soon drafted into the Army. Following his discharge, he continued working for the Army as a civilian for the next forty years. Following the renowned Peter Principle, he was promoted from his successes in the laboratory to a desk job researching questions asked by others, and then he was promoted to a supervisory position. This job supported his family better, but which he never liked as well. However, he had a wife and three children to support. His job with the government was the kind of secure career that his father had advocated. It paid the bills.

Bob and Helen had plans for their retirement. They planned to sell the house, purchase a mobile home on wheels, an RV, travel around the country for a year and then settle in Florida. The good life was just ahead. Unfortunately those plans were not to be realized. Helen, who was distraught at being diagnosed with non-Hodgkin's lymphoma and suffering from the side effects of the medications she was taking, took her own life at the age of 58. Three years later, Bob and I met. Five years after Helen died, he and I married. All of the kids – his and mine were grown and out of the house. We could plan a future together.

On the critical matters, Bob and I were in agreement from the start. Our matching gold wedding bands are etched with lines, symbolizing that we each came to this relationship no longer virginal and new, but with scars and blemishes from previous encounters with life. We also entered the marriage with hope for a future that we would build together. While we saw each other as partners and playmates, we were committed to respecting one another's personal freedom as well. We decided not to impose ourselves on our spouse's children as parents, but to interact with them as adults, of course being supportive to them as each of us had always been.

What we had not expected was his children's cool reception to their father's remarriage. Neither Bob's children nor my two older ones live in the same state as we, so we understand there was little visiting back and forth. At first, we live in my house in Livingston as his comparable house in Chester stands empty. Bob's daughters resent the fact that I host a sixtieth birthday party for him in Livingston. Then we move to Chester and the daughters resent the fact that we change "their" house. They send Adam to inspect the improvements we make and he reports back, "They're only updating the house." Lauren complains when we remove several trees to make the yard larger, that we had disinterred "Floppy" from his/her resting place.

The daughters accept all the furniture we give them, and we drive station wagons full of their mother's possessions to them in Virginia as well. Each of Bob's children then marries and in time each daughter gives birth to a daughter. Adam and his wife have two daughters. We travel each time a child is born to devote a week or two to help care for the mothers and the newborns. We hoped the relationships would improve, but they didn't. No harsh words are spoken, but they keep us at a long distance, especially now that their father is ill.

So Bob and I could develop our lives in our own way. I opened a suburban psychology practice in Chester, New Jersey at Bob's urging. When Bob retired, he could refine his taste in food, both by preparing new recipes or by exploring new restaurants. He could indulge his taste in art films through research and attendance. I took pleasure in his interest in music. A highlight for the two of us was attending a performance of Mozart's Don Juan at the Metropolitan Opera House. We visited museums, traveled and felt full of life. We were always tender and loving with each other, delighting in our good fortune. I feel grateful for the years we have had exploring together. We were both so fortunate – and we knew it.

But now that Bob's memory, reasoning and general functioning are impaired, he has in many ways reverted to the young boy who felt overprotected and poor. He no longer wants to hold my hand when walking in the street. He knows that he is dependent on me to find his way home if we are out of our neighborhood. He prefers to walk behind me. When I ask him about this change, he tells me, "I like to watch the way your body looks from the rear." He feels more independent following me than walking beside me. He does not like me caring for him in any way. "I can make an omelet when I'm hungry" is his way of stating that he can still take care of himself.

The same man who took so much pleasure from choosing from a menu now often finds choice daunting. Bob's ability to choose from a menu varies. On days he seems more together, we try to go to a diner to eat. There he can choose what he wants. Not infrequently, however, he will criticize the food preparation or the serving size or the presentation. I always tell him he can take home whatever isn't finished, so he doesn't feel wasteful, but I end up throwing the food out, as he cannot remember having ordered it. Serving it to him the next day reminds him of a negative feeling.

If I say, "I am going to the park," Bob might answer, "I'll go with you." This is a positive free choice, where "Let's go for a walk to the park" isn't. Of course I also have to be prepared to hear a negative response. "So go. I'll be here when you get back. I'm not going anywhere." If he chooses to join me, he will say, once we are out in the street, "Which park are you going to?" *Not we.* I then have to be specific and not ask his opinion.

"Turn right, we'll go see the sunset over the river." Or "Turn left, we'll walk to the reservoir in Central Park." If I say, "Go straight. I want to stop at Gristede's market," Bob will answer, "Why do two of us need to go there? I can go there by myself. Just give me the list of what you want."

Bob's complaints about my choices, which are inevitable these days, are again assertions of his need for freedom. Although he has lost the ability to choose for himself, and his compliance makes him feel as he did when he was a child, opposing me by criticizing *my* choices helps him feel independent.

I think I have also figured out the reasons behind his paranoid fear of my spending all "his" money. It is only since his wife died, that Bob has been free of money concerns. By the time he and I met, his house was fully paid for, his children were out of college and he finally had discretionary income to spend. Together, we have built up retirement funds and we are debt free – a reassuring situation for us both. Bob invested our money wisely, allowing him – and us – to feel "like a millionaire". What that means is that we own two homes and that he can purchase whatever he wants. Of course coming from Bob's background, his wants are for a new gadget or tool, or a two dollar tee shirt, but still, we are talking about emotions here. But Bob no longer has a sense of monetary values. He has reverted to his childhood concept of prices.

"It used to cost a nickel to ride the subway," he says. Luckily we have Metro Cards, where we just slide the plastic card through the turnstile slot. Otherwise, he would balk at paying for the ride at today's price of $2.25 for regular patrons and $1.25 for seniors.

"For fifteen cents I could get a slice of pizza and a soda," he repeats often.

"I'm not getting any more haircuts. They cost too much money. And the guy wants a tip besides. He's the only person in his shop; he has no other customers waiting. He should be happy I walk in for a ten minute haircut. Twelve dollars? Never," he rants.

He is in charge. He is being decisive. He is exerting control over his life. When Bob sees me spending money, no matter how much, he does not feel in control of anything, which frightens him. In a restaurant, since his memory problems began, he will hand his credit card to the waiter and when the bill arrives, he will add ten percent for a tip. I was thinking he was being miserly and arguing with him, but he's not. It's the only way he can now calculate. Even with that short cut, he's making mistakes. The waiter in the Chinese restaurant comes running down the street after us one evening. "You made a mistake adding the numbers," he says.

Bob has to get used to me paying for our meals out, which no longer seems to bother him. Purchasing something from a list is okay, too. But he gets enraged if I purchase an item at a street fair, or pick something from a shelf which is not on the list. He is afraid I will not exercise the same control on my spending as he does on his. And just perhaps, he is treating me as he was treated as a child when he was told there wasn't enough money to purchase something his parents thought was frivolous, like a replacement football.

13 – Tangles and Plaques

Arizona, November 2009

We return uneventfully to Arizona, in time for Halloween. By November Bob starts in again. "I need to see a lawyer. How does anyone find a lawyer here? We don't even have a phone book in this house. Why is there no phone book here?"

Bob now begins to let me know what has been bothering him. "Why does your son want me to make a wooden house for his turtle to live in?" Bob must be having a problem with the project he is constructing in his garage workshop. "Why doesn't he make one himself if he wants one so badly?"

Last winter, Bob was busy constructing wooden jewelry boxes. This fall, he is no longer able to measure and saw accurately, so Steve has come up with a project for them to do together. They will build a wooden box, two feet wide by four feet long, which will be attached to wrought iron legs Steve has left over from another project. It will have a wood-framed screened cover with hinges and a platform under which the turtle can hide from the sun. It will have a fluorescent light to keep the turtle warm on chilly Arizona nights.

On Sunday, the two men travel by car to Home Depot to purchase the wood, hinges, screws and whatever else they will need, plus waterproof paint to seal the wood. Bob has lined the floor of the garage with paper. The frame is nailed together already, but the legs are not yet attached. I see it in the garage on my way from my car into the house.

"And why is he eating here so often?" Bob goes on. "Why doesn't he eat his own food? All of you are just waiting for me to die so your children can move into this house."

Bob's delusional spiel is off and running. He continues, "And do you know what Grant did?"

I fall into the trap. *Our six year old grandson? What is his transgression?* "No, what did Grant do?" I ask although I know I shouldn't.

"He was here with his father. You weren't home. His father borrowed a box cutter from the closet. He was opening a box from something else you must have bought. And do you know what? Grant wanted to help him. He got another box cutter off the shelf and brought it over to where his father was working."

"Then what happened?" I ask. "Did anyone get hurt?"

"No, if I hadn't been watching, something could have. His father didn't even yell at him. He could have gotten cut. It would have been my fault. They would have blamed me." Bob is extremely agitated. The whole world is against him.

"That was pretty scary," I say. "I see how upset you are. Luckily you were there and nothing bad happened." I have been advised, by Marilynn, by the caregiver's course on managing challenging behaviors and I know from my own experience, that I must speak to Bob's emotions, to how Bob is feeling, not to the specifics of his complaint. I have also been advised not to defend the action, either, so I don't remind Bob that Dave would have said something to his son if he thought the boy was in danger.

"Grant is not allowed in the garage anymore," Bob continues. "Is that clear?" My sentence did not calm him. Bob continues, "When he comes for a visit, they should tie him to a chair so he can't go roaming all over, getting into trouble." Bob's voice grows louder, his words faster. "And one more thing. I don't want your children coming to this house any time they want to; I don't want you feeding them all the time. They have their own houses." *What is at the core of his anger? I see its basis is anxiety, worry about a child he loves.* He calms down for a while.

Our appointment with Dr. L., the neurologist at St. Joseph's Hospital in Phoenix, is on Friday. I try to have patience until we can see the doctor and adjust Bob's medications. Only medication can reduce this agitation. There is no sense reasoning or convincing him of anything.

The next day Bob decides to sell the house. "I walked up the block to the sales office," he tells me. Since it is more than a year since we bought this house, there is no one there who knows Bob except for the sales person who sold us the house who must have been out of the office when Bob arrived. "They couldn't tell me how to get a lawyer to sell this house."

I am shocked and a bit embarrassed that Bob is out in the community showing the world his disability. I have still not fully understood that I cannot manage his behavior and that I am not responsible for how he behaves. The doorbell rings. When I answer the bell, there is a real estate agent who hands me his card and informs me that Bob has called him to speak with him about selling our home.

"I am so glad you are here, Phyllis," he says, "as I need to speak with both of you." This guy would have been a great Fuller brush salesman.

Just as I call Bob, the doorbell rings again. Larry, a caregiver I have just hired to spend the afternoon with Bob, enters the kitchen at the same time as Bob. The agent moves to shake Bob's hand, but Bob does not respond.

"I didn't call a real estate agent, I called a lawyer," says Bob in an agitated voice. "What is going on here?"

Larry intercedes. "Let Phyllis handle this," he tells Bob calmly. "Let's you and me go to the Village Inn for some *huevos rancheros.*" Larry ushers Bob out the front door and into his pick-up truck. What good luck it was to find Larry's name on the bulletin board at the gym! He knows just the right thing to say. Bob goes along, still talking about lawyers and divorces and selling the house.

Finally it is Friday and we see Dr. L. He asks Bob how he likes Arizona, and gets the full force of Bob's allegiance to New York. Dr. L. teases Bob a little and begins to see the agitation I fear. After he examines Bob, he says,

"Your husband has been taking Sinemet to assist in his gait, his posture and his balance. I am going to reduce the medication from three times a day to twice a day, as the medication sometimes causes the agitation you are seeing. If the agitation subsides, don't reduce it further, but if it doesn't, reduce to once a day, or none, changing each week, until you see improvement. If you notice any tremors, or if your husband trips or falls, call me."

What? This miracle is a dud, too? What's going on here?

"Dr. L.," I begin, "Could you please prescribe an alternate medication for agitation? The Xanax is not controlling his outbursts or his anxiety." He agrees to prescribe 25 mg Seroquel to be taken up to three times a day. Our next visit to the doctor is scheduled one month later.

14 – Children Visit

Arizona, January-February 2010

All of a sudden, it is January again, but now in 2010, Bob has another rageful outburst.

In the morning one day, while I am at the gym, Bob calls his friend Eliot, in New Jersey. I then get a call from Adam telling me about the phone call, adding that they are concerned because Bob is asking for help in getting a divorce.

"And what have you told him, Adam?" I ask.

"Well, frankly, Phyllis, he is still my father. And I have to follow his wishes. As you said once, I will do what my father wants me to do," he pompously responds, clearly not understanding the ranting of a demented person. This is almost the same sentence Adam used in January, 2008, when Adam suggested we find an assisted living apartment for his father. It is two years later now. I tell Adam about the recent neurology visit and the follow-up visit which is scheduled in two weeks. Perhaps he would like to speak with the neurologist himself, since he is concerned about his father's health and the care he is receiving.

"I just called to check how he is doing," Adam backs down. He doesn't want the doctor's number or name. Whenever Bob's illness causes him to feel paranoid or to become angry with me, it seems like Adam rushes to his father's aid. He is not supportive of his father at any other time.

The next day I get a call from Adam's wife, Sheree.

"Is there a resort near you where we could stay? We're thinking about coming out there over Washington's birthday weekend." Sheree tells me what she has found on the internet. I respond joyfully.

The next day I get a call from Bob's daughter Lauren. "Emily and I want to come out, too. This way Emily can see her cousins. Do you mind if we stay with you?"

"That's fine," I respond. *The troops are gathering for battle.*

I have mixed feelings about this visit. I feel that Adam and his sisters still do not understand that their father is ill. I hope this visit will help them understand dementia better. I worry that my husband's behavior is unpredictable. I don't want them to see him in a rage. *Or do I?* Since Bob has exaggerated the value and the beauty of this 2350 square foot development home, I'm glad they will see for themselves that we live a modest lifestyle. I am angry with myself that I still care what they think. I am delighted Bob will get to see his children and his grandchildren. I miss them, too, and I will enjoy spending time with them. I hope he recognizes them.

I don't tell Bob the family is coming until the day they arrive. In the morning, Bob goes outside via the front door, to collect the New York Times from the driveway. He comes back into the kitchen, exclaiming, "There are people in the guest room. One of them is awake. I can see her feet sticking up. Can I go in and see her?"

"Can you wait until they get up? It's your daughter Lauren and your granddaughter Emily. She's seven. They arrived really late last night and might want a bit more sleep," I answer practically.

A few minutes later, Bob is holding sleepy Emily's hand. He is showing her the house.

"See, here is the kitchen, and here is Grandma and my bedroom. If we go this way, we can go outside into the back yard." Bob turns toward me.

"Her sister is still sleeping, but this one woke up." he says explaining his actions. *Oops, he's got the relationship wrong.*

Emily looks adorable in her Valentine's Day pajamas, pink with red hearts all over. She speaks in a mini-voice and not very often. She is very compliantly walking around with her grandfather, whom she hasn't seen for 18 months. When asked if she'd like some food or drink, she shyly says, "No, thank you." Bob and Emily exit toward his room and the garage.

"Good morning," I say. It's Lauren, sleepy in pajamas.

"Where's Dad and Emily?" she responds.

"They must be out in the garage or in Dad's room. She's fine," I answer. Exit Lauren.

Lauren returns, dressed in shorts and sneakers and asks, "Is it safe to walk around the block? Emily and I want to see the neighborhood."

"Sure." I answer her. "Dad may want to come with you. Why don't you ask him to join you?"

I go for a walk by myself since Lauren is with her father and Lauren hasn't said hello to me or made any other friendly gesture. At least I can get a few minutes to myself. When I return, Emily and Lauren are eating

107

English muffins. Bob is reading the paper on the patio. When I ask if her father has had his breakfast, Lauren says, "Dad said he wasn't hungry." *She doesn't see he needs direction?*

I prepare Bob's breakfast, set out his medications, make coffee and call him in. Emily and Lauren leave to shower and dress. I take out a 300 piece large- sized jigsaw puzzle and lay the pieces out on the card table in the corner of the living room. Perhaps we will have a collaborative puzzle building effort, or not. I go to shower and dress. Then it's Bob's turn. So now we are all dressed. Bob reads his paper, Emily draws and Lauren reads a magazine. *What is wrong with this picture?* Lauren hasn't said hello to me, she has not commented on the house and she is not visiting with her father.

I walk into my office, check my email, and call Linda.

"Mom," she says, "Remember what you always tell me. When someone disappoints you, lower your expectations." By one o'clock, the phone rings. It's Adam. They're here. What do I want them to do?

"Why don't you come over? We'll figure stuff out when you get here," I suggest. We hang up. We wait for them to arrive. He calls back an hour later.

"We decided to go to the hotel and unpack first. Where would you like to have dinner?"

I suggest a place and start to give him driving directions.

"You're giving me driving directions? I have a GPS. We'll find it."

We meet at 5:30 at an Italian family-friendly restaurant where I have made a reservation. After the cousins greet each other and Emily decides she wants to sit near Gabby, we are seated at a long table. As at their home, the three adults are seated at one end of the table, Bob and I at the other. Bob sees his grandchildren, but he does not interact with them. We eat quietly. After dinner, Sheree comes to our side of the table, switching seats with Emily. She looks directly at Bob and talks with him. He smiles and talks to her, but tells her it is too noisy to have a conversation in the restaurant. He's right. We were here early, when it was not crowded. Now it is.

We leave and go home. It takes Adam a bit longer to find the development. He doesn't follow me, and of course the development is too new to be on his GPS. Sheree enters and is exuberant. "What a great house," she 'oohs' and 'ahs', complimenting the house, the back yard, the high ceilings, the color scheme, the large kitchen, Bob's office and she even praises his tool collection.

Steve arrives with Pebbles, his dachshund, which enlivens the scene for a while. Lauren completes the puzzle with Emily seated on her lap.

Adam and his family leave, promising to return the next day in the afternoon to swim at our brand-new community pool. I have invited Linda, Dave and Grant to join Ted, Steve and the rest of us for a whole family gathering. I have ordered Mexican food for dinner for all in honor of Ted, Adam and Dave who all have birthdays this week, plus it is Valentine's Day, so I have stuff for the kids. Austin comes for dinner, too.

Bob keeps missing someone. His daughter Alison is not here. Whenever he sees his two granddaughters, Jess and Gabby, he wants to say Lauren and Alison, but he knows that's wrong.

When he sees Lauren and Emily, he calls them sisters. He is confused, but quiet. Lauren busies herself with Emily; Sheree is very helpful as is Linda getting the food out. The children play with the dog. Dave watches television. Adam and Steve try to talk. No one talks to Bob.

Steve reports later, "Mom, Adam tried to thank me for being nice to his father. I'm not doing anything for Adam. Whatever we do for Bob, we do because we love him and we love you. Really, we are helping you."

On Sunday, Bob's family piles into Adam's rented minivan and we drive into the mountains, so they can see something of Arizona. No one is really interested. We eat lunch at a Superstition Mountain golf resort. The cousins chat with each other. The adults eat quietly. We drive to the resort in Scottsdale where Adam and his family are staying, because the girls want to go swimming there. The adults have drinks near the pool, watching the cousins swim. We drive to another restaurant for dinner.

"I don't know what I want to eat," says Bob. "Nothing interests me here."

"Would you like a bowl of soup?" I ask as I point to the menu.

"Okay," says Bob without enthusiasm. Jess is upset and doesn't eat. Adam is angry with Jess for not participating. Sheree's steak arrives improperly cooked. She sends it back and we wait forever for a new order. They drive us back 45 minutes from Scottsdale to Mesa and return to their hotel. Monday morning they depart. We drive Emily and Lauren to the airport.

"Thanks for the ride," Lauren says. They leave as well. I guess they've seen that life is ordinary here, their father is confused and he has mood swings.

Nothing was ever discussed with me. No questions were asked about divorce. This becomes a very important visit because, in May, when Bob has another frightening episode, Adam phones me and says, "Dad called me, very upset. I tried to calm him, but he's probably forgotten already. I know he is incompetent." Wow, he finally understands. *At least I hope so.*

15 – Time Changes

New York, April 2010

Time is relative, explained Einstein. As a caregiver to a demented spouse, every idea I ever had about time, changes. In the beginning, I had expectations merely of a slow decline in memory function as was the case with my mother's illness. But I did not know that my husband would sleep many more hours per day. Further, I did not know that his lack of a sense of time would make him unable to tell the difference between day and night. Of course he expects me to be up with him. So I have to set a rule. I am not to be wakened before 7 a.m. unless it's an emergency. I move the clock radio to his side of our bed. Wherever he is in our home, my husband remembers to come into bed for his hugs and cuddle time at 7 a.m. Again it is amazing, what he remembers and what he forgets.

I have traveled this landscape before, when my mother was diagnosed with Alzheimer's disease. But each case is different and each person's response is different. The progression of the disease and its manifestations vary from one Alzheimer's sufferer to another. I do know this: it is better to discover what you are dealing with sooner rather than later. That way, you can take advantage of certain medications that may slow the disease's progression.

Looking back, it is clear to me that my mother had been experiencing memory problems for at least four years prior to her diagnosis. But I didn't see it, or at least I chose not to. Probably both. Like so many children of aging parents, I no longer lived near my mother, nor did I see her often, as I was busy with my own life. In 1990, when Bob and I were married, my mother was 78. She seemed fine, taught nursery school every morning, played mah jong and canasta with her friends every week, attended New Jersey Philharmonic concerts in Newark every month and drove her Chevy Impala faster than I ever did. My younger son, Ted, and his friends called her "Speedy Gonzales."

From 1976, when my father died, my mother and I were very close. My first husband and I had divorced four years earlier. Mom and I traveled together and attended family functions as a couple. Beginning in 1984, she was the bookkeeper for my psychology practice. I "paid" her with tickets to the New York Philharmonic Orchestra season, which we attended together. By 1989, I met Bob and was caught up in a new romance. I had a job in Coney Island, the famous beach resort on the south side of Brooklyn which is now very rundown; I was trying to grow my private practice in Manhattan and I was traveling back and forth to be with Bob in New Jersey. So yes, I saw less of my mother. But although we spoke every day, I distanced myself a bit from her. After the marriage, when she phoned at 8 a.m. on a Saturday morning, I thought she was being insensitive. I was still employed in Coney Island at the time and I was driving many miles each week. Mom started worrying because she began to listen to the traffic reports in the morning.

"What is rubbernecking?" she called to ask one morning. "They're doing that on the BQE."

"Will you be near the Cross Island Expressway? There is an accident there," she reported. I was surprised at these early morning phone calls, but thought nothing amiss.

Unbeknownst to me, my mother was locking herself out of her car frequently and phoning my younger sister to rescue her. Sharyn and I are not on good terms so I did not hear of these things until later. One day however, I received a call from Aunt Lisa, my mother's sister-in-law. "Phyllis, your mother was supposed to come to Livingston to visit me, and she's not here," she said. "Where do you think she could be?"

I didn't know. Aunt Lisa finally reached my mother several hours later. Mom told her, "I changed my mind and decided not to come." When I spoke to her at home, Mom finally admitted that she had set out for Aunt Lisa's house, gotten lost and found her way home instead. I listened but still it didn't register as something to check out.

Visiting my mother on another day, I opened the refrigerator and discovered several two liter bottles of soda on the shelves. She had never bought so much soda before. Indeed she rarely drank soda. When asked, Mom said, "I had a coupon." My Mom always shopped with coupons, traveling to three different super markets to get special sales. But she only purchased what she ate or drank. *This looks random to me. Do I do anything about it? No.*

Two years later, in 1992, the director of the nursery school phoned Sharyn and asked if my mother was planning to retire at the end of the year. If not, she told her, they were planning to ask her to leave. I knew since the fall term started that she was having problems remembering the children's names. I suggested she ask the children to leave their September name tags on all year. Mom also had trouble remembering the words to the songs she sang with the children. So I asked a friend of mine, who is a nursery school director, to print out the lyrics to the songs. My mom knew how to play the songs on the piano without sheet music. *Was this normal aging? I wanted to think so.*

Sharyn, Aunt Lisa and I finally put all the pieces together and realized that Mom should not be driving anymore and that something was wrong. Still we did nothing. We were afraid she'd be angry if we asked her to stop driving and tell us it was none of our business. So Mom continued to drive even after she retired from teaching that spring.

One evening the following December, Bob was away on a business trip; my Mom and I went out to dinner and to a movie. I drove. When we returned to her home, I parked the car, and got out to walk her to the front door. She refused. "It's late," she insisted. "You have a 45 minute ride home. I am perfectly capable of walking up the path to my door. You don't have to walk me." She had her keys in her hand. So I waited with the headlights illuminating her path until she reached her apartment and opened the screen door. The porch light was on. She waved me on, and I drove home. I arrived to a ringing phone. It was my mother.

"The heel of my shoe got stuck in the door frame, and I fell and hit my head," she told me.

"Are you bleeding?"

"No, but my head hurts and I feel dizzy," she reported. I phoned Sharyn and she called 911. Mom was taken to the emergency room, then to stay with Sharyn and her family until a home health aide was hired to assist Mom at home. Sharyn then scheduled an appointment for our mother to be evaluated at the Daughters of Israel Geriatric Center and we drove to the appointment together. We sat flanking our mother as the social worker asked questions.

"Do you know what day it is?"

"It's Wednesday," Mom replied. Sharyn's eyebrows went up in a questioning look. It was not Wednesday. The social worker looked at Sharyn. "You may only remain in the room if you promise not to make any indication of right or wrong answers," she said. I am shocked as I see how much is missing from our mother's memory. *This is an eye opener for me.* Mom did not know the name of the president of the United States, she did not remember the three items mentioned by the social worker (box, hat, ball) when she was asked for recall.

But still, as we passed the day care center for Alzheimer's patients on our way to the parking lot, Sharyn and I agreed, "This is not a place for Mom. She doesn't belong here, except maybe as a volunteer." By the following September, Mom was picked up by the van every morning after her aide got her ready, and she spent the days joyfully at the center.

A spouse sees early signs sooner than an adult child. But the sentence "Denial (De Nile) is a wide river" applies to all. We don't see what we don't want to see until something forces us to face the reality. The physicians never really say it is Alzheimer's disease. They say that people who have problems with tasks of daily living, feeding themselves, dressing themselves, bathing themselves or using the bathroom appropriately are at the stage of decline commonly seen as Moderate Alzheimer's disease. That was my mother's diagnosis.

My sister becomes the caregiver, supervising the aides, shopping, paying the bills. I'm busy with my new husband and my psychology practice. We begin traveling and in 1993, when my husband retires, we commute between our New York and New Jersey residences. We visit Mom and Yvonne, the aide who lived with my mother for five years, every Sunday. My friend Barbara, who had been a nurse, often comes along, or substitutes for my husband. We watch my mother's gradual decline; she lost the most recently learned information first, although she did not remember how to speak German which, being her native language, I thought would survive longer.

Gail Sheehy, in her book "Passages in Care-Giving", states that the average length of time as a caregiver is five years. My mother died eight years after her Moderate Alzheimer's Disease diagnosis. My husband's initial diagnosis was Mild Cognitive Impairment because we both recognized the symptoms sooner and could avail ourselves of medication to slow the progression of this illness. In April 2010, the neurologist declared, "I don't know what I am treating, but it seems to be working for now."

It is today four years after my husband's initial neurology consult and my husband is approximately at the same level of forgetfulness as my mother was when she was first diagnosed. I feel sure that, being married, Bob had a better chance of getting an early diagnosis and early treatment options. And I truly believe that the medications he has been receiving have slowed the progress of his memory loss.

But I also recognize how easy it is to deny the early symptoms of Alzheimer's disease.

For example: Bob's niece Jeannie arrives for dinner at Uncle Bobby's invitation. He thinks about her again because, on a bus ride to Second Avenue, Bob suddenly remarks, "I have a niece who lives around here someplace." After dinner, which is uneventful, Jeannie says, "I think sometimes Uncle Bobby is pulling the wool over our eyes. Do you think he could be faking this illness? Sometimes he sounds and looks so with it, and then he will tell the same story over again as if we had not just heard it." I feel like that myself sometimes, Jeannie, he has these sudden moments of clarity, but they do not last.

A person with Alzheimer's disease no longer has a sense of time regulated by a clock. My husband's sense of time is now regulated by his stomach. He doesn't feel hungry at mealtime, but he would rather graze any time of the 24 hour cycle. He doesn't want to shower and dress in the morning, or even in the early afternoon. "I'm not going anywhere," he says when asked. But even if he is to go somewhere, he doesn't remember. So I write him notes. He keeps the calendar by his desk, and crosses off the days, until he forgets about it. Or, he uses the newspaper to tell him the date. He doesn't really care what day it is, or what time of day. "It doesn't matter," he says. Perhaps it doesn't. *Perhaps it matters to me, as he says, because I want to control him. He feels I find fault with him at every opportunity.*

Perhaps his sense of taste and smell are affected by this disease. Because when a meal is put in front of him, he either rejects it outright, eats none of it, or he devours the whole plateful, more than he was accustomed to eating before this illness. Nothing is stable, nothing is predictable and nothing stays the same for very long.

16 – Tenacity

New York, April 2010

The role of caregiver to a spouse with this difficult and unpredictable illness, diagnosed as both Alzheimer's disease and Parkinson's disease is the toughest challenge I have ever faced. With the change in diagnosis and a subsequent change in medications, my spouse has been coherent, lucid, and generally happy for a month. We have also returned to New York. The change perks him up, too. Then, Bob experiences some bedwetting problems. We go first to our internist where the urinalysis shows no infection, then for a sonogram and a consult with a specialist in urinary tract problems. The evaluation also shows no reason for the incontinence. A prescription is ordered and Bob takes the medication for a month with no letup of the symptoms. I handle it all without judging him. I change sheets, buy two different kinds of absorbent supplies, wash and soothe him when accidents occur. Otherwise, Bob is responding so well, I reduce his agitation medication from three times a day to once, at bedtime, to help him sleep. (No, it didn't cause the bedwetting. I checked.) I still don't understand that the medication has to be taken as ordered. It does no one any good to reduce medication for any reason. *Why do I always have to learn everything the hard way?*

At the neurologist's office, the doctor was so pleased he said he didn't need to see my husband again for three months. We go out to lunch to celebrate. Bob enjoys the lunch in a quiet Italian restaurant and the bus rides. He's communicative as we hold hands walking on the street. And today, due to two mistakes on my part, his equilibrium is destroyed and so is mine.

First, I reduce a medication that controls his anxiety. Second, we receive a check in the mail for a bond that was called. I assume Bob will be pleased.

"Bob," I say, "The check came for the bond that was called. It's made out to you. Please sign it and we'll go to the bank to deposit it, okay?"

"Do you want me to go with you?" he asks.

"Sure. We'll go for a little walk. I have to stop at Gristede's," I answer.

"Okay, we need fruit." he says.

We go to the bank first. Bob watches me deposit the check in the ATM machine. The supermarket is next.

"I'll go get pears," Bob says when we enter, walking into the first aisle.

"Okay, meet me in the household supplies aisle," I answer and head there.

Bob soon joins me in the aisle where I am shopping; he's carrying three pears. I am delighted and pleased that he selected the right fruit and that he remembered where to find me. *Look how well he is doing. I feel proud.*

"What are you buying new sponges for? What's the matter with the sponge you have? Why are you spending money on sponges? What ARE you DOING to me?" Bob starts yelling in the market. I look around to see who has heard this.

Quietly I say, "Anna left me a note." Anna is our housekeeper. "I'm buying the things on her list." I show Bob the list. "Why do you need a new sponge? What's wrong with the one you have? Why are you always buying things? You are spending my money foolishly. I don't know what you are doing to me." He repeats himself in the aisle, at the checkout counter, all the way home.

Once inside the apartment, he really screams at me. There is no way to reason with him when he's like this. Actually, there is no way to reason with Bob anymore. His ability to reason is destroyed. I don't know how to diffuse this situation. Perhaps if I walk out of the room, he will calm down. Outwardly, I remain calm, and I leave the room.

"Go, leave the room," he shouts, following me. "Leave the house, why don't you? I don't need you. I can do fine here without you."

"No, Bob," I say, "I am not leaving. I love you. I know you are upset. We'll talk about this a little later." I try to stay calm.

"I am perfectly capable of taking care of myself," he repeats. "And anyway, if I want company there are plenty of ladies at the synagogue who would love to live here with me."

I go into the kitchen and prepare supper.

"I'm not hungry. I will make myself an omelet when I'm ready," he yells.

"I am not going anywhere," I repeat quietly. "I love you and I will always be with you." I eat my dinner and turn on the news.

I am quietly fuming. Marilynn, who attends a weekly Alzheimer's spousal support group, reminds me often, "Talk to the illness. Don't take what he says personally. If you are furious it is because you still haven't given up the false hope that he can be well. Your husband is a sick man and he will not get better. Don't be fooled by occasional upswings in mood or behavior."

The social workers at the Alzheimer Association also say to enjoy the good times and not to be so disappointed when things don't go so well. *How easy it all sounds. Advice always sounds easy to the person giving it.*

So what kind of advice am I giving you, my reader? My husband IS capable of making himself an omelet. So what if he has an omelet every day for a while, and then he has bologna sandwiches for lunch until the package is used up?

Why did I give up my psychology practice to wait on this man? Yes, he asked me to. He said he felt uncomfortable being in the house alone. He couldn't find the things he needs. His first wife died of cancer at age fifty-eight. She had asked him to retire from his work and care for her. He agitated over the decision, but finally decided he could not do it. He would lose his life's work, she would die; he would lose again and not be able to find comparable scientific work later.

I was seventy years old when the same question was asked of me. It was a reasonable retirement age. We did have enough money for me to retire. In addition, I had committed myself to a delusion that I could keep Bob healthy for a long time. In order to accomplish that high goal, I had to prepare in advance. I had to have a handi-cap-accessible home for the time when the Parkinson's worsens. I had to prevent him from ever having to go to a nursing home. I had to have a safe place for him to be, if he starts wandering. I wanted my children around me, so I could have some help caring for him. Bob's children would be satisfied to have their father in an assisted living home already. They don't visit, or write or even phone. Their father's illness is too difficult for them to process.

I do not accept defeat lightly. I will persevere. Somewhere I have confused not giving up with not be-ing able to let go. "Persistent," "cohesive"," adhesive" and "retentive" are all definitions of the adjective tena-cious. I just looked it up. I am extremely tenacious. I can and will stay the course; I can and will keep it all togeth-er. I will not abandon Bob but I cannot keep him or me or the relationship the way it was, or the way I would like it to be.

17 – Insight

New York, April 2010

I am seated at a table next to my friend, Marilynn, who is also a spousal caregiver to a demented husband. Only she has been married for the past fifty-one years to my mere twenty. Her husband was diagnosed with Lewy-Body dementia about a year earlier than Bob. Norman needs dialysis treatment three times a week. To help her cope, Marilynn attends a weekly support group for well spouses. In turn, she helps me cope. She has been my go-to person for support these past two years.

Marilynn tells me about this conference for caregivers, being held at the library of the Academy of Medicine. I walk there from my apartment on the west side of Central Park. I leave my husband home alone so I can attend this conference. I am so overwhelmed by my responsibility to take care of my husband, whose illness changes every few months, that I ask, review, read, listen to anything that could be helpful. Yet, I am so sensitized to my performance, that I feel as if I am being criticized for not doing enough to solve this problem. Besides, I have attended and given more workshops, conferences and presentations during my twenty-five year career than I care to count. So, the last thing I want is to be here, listening to "professionals" telling me how to take care of my spouse. I feel defensive and frightened of what I am about to hear. I don't need any more advice, or criticism, for that matter. But Marilynn has asked me to come, and to support her, I comply.

After what seems like an interminable time the program begins. There are seven speakers seated at the head of the room, caregivers as well as doctors and researchers. Each of the first three panelists shares her experience of caring for an aging parent. They speak of bureaucratic difficulty combined with personal grief, time issues, and money problems, issues with identifying and accessing needed services. But these are *parents* they are talking about and while I'm sympathetic, the fact is that caring for a spouse is different. Nothing I hear in this hour and a half that I sit here is relevant to me. I am seething. I didn't want to be here before and I cannot sit here a moment longer. I want O-U-T!!!

Then the sponsor, the director of Senior Bridge, calls a ten minute break before the professionals share their stories. I escape. *I still have time to get to a class at the gym.* The gym is on the west side of Central Park at 97th Street. I will walk back across the park, no problem. Day rescued. I will be able to work out these feelings of anger and frustration. I am angry that nothing in the past two wasted hours has anything to do with me. I need help but I did not find it here.

I have had this feeling of impotency before. When my first-born son, Steven was a schoolboy, he encountered difficulties in learning in school. He resorted to bad behavior to get the attention he needed from his friends. They liked his shenanigans, and his flaunting of adult authority. The reports from his teachers concerned his behavior but not the problems he was having writing a report or answering questions on a test in a timely manner.

So then, too I decided to become more educated. I enrolled for a master's degree at Montclair State College. I majored in psychology with a concentration in learning disabilities. I read, I attended workshops then, too, and over the years I was able to assist many families with similar problems. But I was unable then as now, to get meaningful ideas for a solution I could use with my own family member immediately. *So, what exactly did I expect to find out*? As I walk in the park, the questions form in my mind. I want to know what is expected of me. I want to know what to do, what to expect, how to plan, how to wrap my mind around this life I am living. The idea of vague diagnoses, complaints about accessing government-paid help, stories of how stressed women are with all their multiple work and family issues is not what I need.

I remember seeking direction last winter when I enrolled in a ten-week caregiver workshop in Arizona. We role played dealing with insensitive family members, we role played dealing with spouses who exhibit "challenging" behaviors; we were given lists of agencies that we could consult to help with THE DECISION. And what is this big decision? In the winter course as in today's presentation, the decision is when to place the patient in one of the sponsor's day or residential care facilities.

Okay, so now I know why I am angry. None of my questions were being addressed at this morning's event. And the sponsor of the program is yet another organization whose business is providing long term care facilities

127

for the aged and ailing. I have promised myself that I will never send my spouse to a nursing home. I may not be able to keep that promise. I continue to walk. But I get no closer to the exit on the west side of the park. I realize I have gotten myself lost in Central Park. I cannot find which way is west. I end up in the North Woods. No one is around who can help me. I look at the time on my cell phone. It is noon. No wonder, even the sun can't help me. It is too late for my class. I just want to get out of the park. I get to an exit. I am on the west side, but at 106th Street, a mile north of my home.

Although the spring day is mild, I am all perspired. I continue to walk west, when I should have just followed Central Park West and headed south. My mind is stuck on the impossibility of my situation. I wander in a maze of hills and streets that are not cross streets.

Finally, I reach Columbus Avenue and begin my descent towards home. I can't believe what a mess I have made of my day and I don't know how to manage the mess of my life. This morning's event, like so many others I've attended, dealt with care-giving, all right, but their agendas do not match with my reality. I review the morning as I walk. The program sponsors have targeted a group of likely customers: mostly women caring for their elderly parents. They will more than likely need to place their parents in one of the sponsor's residential care facilities in the future. In attendance are also social workers and others who advise them. Suddenly I realize more of what is causing this huge response in me. These women do not have to live with the person for whom they are providing care. *They can go home.* They can have a life. They don't cook or clean, but they pay bills for their parent. They hire caregivers. They accompany the patient to medical appointments. They order medications. They deal with insurance companies. *But they get to go home.* They experience frustration, they have legitimate concerns. They are not just whining. I feel their pain. *But they get to go home. I don't get that kind of break. I have lost the partner who shared my life.*

I am a second wife. Although I love my husband dearly, he is not the father of my children. We don't have the history of Marilynn and her husband with their two children. Bob has three children, two daughters and a son. They seem oblivious to the changes their father's illness have brought to our lives and offer no help or support. I have given up a lot in the past two years. I have given up my psychology practice. I have given up our Row N center Saturday evening subscription seats to the New York Philharmonic at Avery Fisher Hall which I have held since 1980. We have stopped traveling to Europe every August. We have stopped having conversation – our interchanges are reduced to the voicing of queries and commands. "Where did you put my slippers?" "Take your morning pills, please." I find myself slowing down, literally, to accommodate my husband's pace and to satisfy his need for exercise. I plan outings that will please him, not me. He loves only thrift stores and 99 cent stores where he can purchase more tools or knives. We can now only attend movies that aren't subtitled, without flashbacks. Our favorite art films are a thing of the past as are the fancy restaurants Bob used to choose. My gourmet cook prefers diner food, now.

He will eat only chicken. Most of our friends have stopped inviting us. We still have a close knit group of people who eat at home with us and invite us to their homes. The table conversations are stilted if he is quiet and a monologue if he is in a story telling mood.

I am getting closer to our home. I am tired, thirsty and hungry, but I am reluctant to end this walk. I feel freer out here on the street. I stop at a farmer's market. I calm myself down. I understand my rage. And then it hits me again, from the inside this time. I CAN do the same thing. I can have a life and Bob CAN still enjoy the things that still give him pleasure. I can hire a companion here in New York to go on those boring outings. Bob likes to stand and watch the ConEd electrical and gas technicians dig up the streets. Bob likes to visit thrift stores. I don't. Bob likes to travel to parts of the city where he used to live, or where his grandparents lived. They are in rundown parts of the city. I will not go there. He can't go alone.

I can still do some good in the world. I can tell others about this experience in time for them to save themselves. The caregiver gives up a year of her life for every year she spends care-giving full time. I can take a class. I can attend a Philharmonic concert or a play with friends without Bob if I choose.

This was the most important conference I have ever attended. It is now several weeks later. I feel free. I bask in the knowledge of my release from self-imposed burdens. People come up to me and ask why I look so much better. I think they want to know if I've had face-lift surgery. I am smiling more. I am happier. It is weird. My husband's behavior hasn't changed. He still has mood swings. He still calls me names once in a while. But my attitude has changed. I have hired two helpers who each arrive twice a week. One man, a neighbor, invites my husband out to lunch. They are together perhaps two hours. The other is hired to spend four hours twice weekly going on an outing. The woman who cleans our apartment is here the fifth afternoon. I can write, do errands alone or just sit in the park and read.

My physical health has improved as well, but the physical and psychological trauma of this responsibility affects the caregiver in so many more ways than I could ever have imagined. I am generally a healthy person. Yet, soon after Bob was diagnosed, I began to experience uncontrollable diarrhea. I would have to hurry home, or stop in at Gristede's and ask to use their basement worker's bathroom. I worried about unsightly accidents. Sometimes I didn't make it on time. First I thought I had the flu. Then I figured out I had given myself Irritable Bowel Syndrome. At my annual physical checkup, when my physician asked how I had been feeling during the past year, I burst into tears. I told her of my husband's illness, how he was depressed and how I was feeling responsible for everything in our lives. She suggested perhaps I was not getting enough fiber in my diet. I left the doctor's office, bought the fiber tablets, knowing that they were not the solution. I became very socially unacceptable, gassy all day long. Problem not resolved. The next year, I was plagued with a skin rash. The dermatologist took a biopsy; luckily, there was no eczema or skin cancer. Creams did not work, but she finally cured the lesions by injecting each with a steroid solution. I went for another annual exam. The internist opined that I might have celiac disease and suggested I go on a wheat free diet. She did this without waiting for the results of a blood test. In the meantime, I developed urinary tract infections and vaginal infections. The gynecologist prescribed creams and antibiotics.

After six months on the wheat-free and dairy free diet, with probiotics and a fiber pill, I began to experience reduced symptoms. But I was also bored with my food limitations. I decided to enroll in Weight Watchers. I needed to lose ten pounds anyway. I am a take charge person and do better when I have a plan. Have more fiber. I can do it. Avoid wheat. I can do that. Lose weight? I can do that as well. Deal with Bob's illness? No one can tell me what to do, no one knows. We caregivers are, each of us, on our own, handling each emotional upheaval as it arrives. Letting go is hard to do. So I decide to substitute a healthier obsession for the unhealthy one. I modify the WW menus to exclude wheat and dairy. The group process works because in Weight Watchers there are solutions for each problem. I was advised about gluten-free products. I utilized their menus. In ten weeks, I accomplished my goal, received my ribbon, and I felt a lot better. I can now even cheat a bit, either with dairy or with wheat and not be sick! Was the extra weight the problem?

Each professional had treated a part of me that was symptomatic. No one treated the whole me, and none of us realized the extent to which the tension of my husband's illness added to my pains. I rationalized my symptoms by using age as a factor. *As we age, systems fail. I am lucky nothing is seriously wrong with me. I am not joining the ranks of those who recite their ailments at lunch.*

I am ready for the conference to let me conclude that while I have to take charge of this changed situation, taking charge need not translate into exclusive management of both of our lives – my husband's and mine. With this understanding, I am ready to strike a healthier balance between my husband's needs as he declines, and mine.

18 – Hired Helpers Saga

April-December 2010

The country mouse and the city mouse have different lives. So too, as a caregiver, life is different in the suburbs where everything is readily available, but only to people who own and can drive a car. In the city, all is available on foot, but generally at higher prices and one must be able to walk confidently and independently. In the beginning of his illness, when Bob still had a sense of monetary values, he preferred shopping in the suburbs and the big box stores. After we moved full time to New York, Bob still preferred to visit New Jersey. We still kept a car in the city, and we did the weekly grocery shopping and occasional clothing shopping on days we were in New Jersey for my practice hours.

In Arizona the closest store is two miles away. At this point, Bob no longer has a sense of what items cost and has no memory of what we paid elsewhere, so we stop any price comparisons and simply buy what he needs, wherever it is most conveniently found. When I get to shop by myself, someday, I will once again shop prices.

With this illness comes a reduction in the ability to delay gratification. When Bob wants something, he wants it now. So, every time he needs some wood or screws or glue or water softener pellets in Arizona, I have to drop whatever I'm doing and drive him the two miles to Home Depot. Steve takes some of the Home

Depot runs when possible, but there are other demands on his time, like work, for instance. It is also true that Bob has become so dependent on me that I feel trapped. I cannot go out to lunch with my daughter. I can't attend a function at my grandchildren's schools. Bob and I are too often together and isolated at the same time.

In the city, initially Bob would walk to Ace Hardware to get a light bulb or picture hooks as soon as he needed them. Of course if he waited, he would forget what he wanted or why. But when I was at my office and Bob couldn't find something we had in the apartment it was very frustrating for him. He did try to help himself, by labeling the cabinets and shelves where things are kept. For example, I found a note on the inside of his closet door that says "iron in cupboard under sink". Bob also made lists of items he wished to accomplish that day. I would see notes Bob wrote to himself "fix shelf in book-case", "buy nails", and "go to library". After a while, those lists and Bob's ability to think of tasks he wished to accomplish faded.

Next, I write lists, including the day and date, informing Bob to take his medications, to shower, to dress and I leave him a small grocery list of items that he could carry home. I make sure to add my telephone number each time. Eventually these lists no longer work and all of these attempts at having Bob remain self-sufficient fail. Bob requires constant attention and I need help.

I try to hire help first in Arizona, but most people working as home care aides are Mexican with little command of the English language and are trained to provide physical assistance to patients who have difficulty managing the tasks of daily living, washing, dressing, toileting, eating. They are kind and generous people who are overworked and underpaid. They need the person they care for to be appreciative of their services. Bob doesn't need hands-on care yet and he is not receptive to assistance of any kind. He needs companionship. He needs a man, preferably of retirement age himself, who is willing to eat diner food for lunch or doughnuts and coffee at mid-afternoon and to accompany Bob to Home Depot, thrift stores and flea markets. Bob still enjoys museums and factory tours. He goes to a micro-brewery, as an example. He can follow the procedure and process the information. Here's the problem. Bob doesn't want to pay for anyone to go with him. He doesn't want me to pay for it either. He wants me to accompany him on these outings. The burden of caring for a man who has no ability to entertain himself and who needs constant supervision is overwhelming for me. I have to have another plan.

Larry – In Arizona

"Bob," I say to my husband one day, "I met a woman at the gym who has a neighbor whose mother died last year. He moved to Arizona to care for her. Now he is all alone and he has no friends. She wants to know if you'd like to meet him." Okay, the part about caring for his mom who died is true. After asking around and much research online, I found a note on the bulletin board at the gym. So the gym part is true, too. It's from a man named Larry who owns a pick-up truck and has a sister who lives in town. Larry is a 66 year old divorced man who is six foot-six inches tall. He has grey hair and a ready, if somewhat shy, smile. He is looking for a companion position, part-time. He is willing to befriend Bob and to meet me at the gym every two weeks to discuss Bob's preferences and attitudes and to get paid. He visits us at home first, and then suggests that he and Bob leave together for a trip to Home Depot. Larry includes lunch in that first outing. Bob agrees.

When they return, Bob says, "That was a good lunch." He also has a bag with him with two brightly-patterned short-sleeved shirts. Since Bob enjoys the outing, I hire Larry for three afternoons each week. He takes Bob to visit the airplane museum or to his sister's home. They generally eat either lunch or a mid-afternoon snack and they shop at thrift stores, flea markets and yard sales.

Larry is a wonderful listener. Bob tells him whatever is on his mind. He even complains to Larry about the "fact" that I am spending ALL his money. Larry listens. Bob and Larry share the same interests. I don't think Bob buys into the ruse that Larry is not being compensated, but I think he plays along because he really enjoys this time with his friend. It's a win for us all.

Barry – In New York

I decide to take a course in Divorce Mediation. I am concerned about the future – what will I do? Hired helpers cost a lot of money. Caring for Bob takes a lot of time. This certification will allow me to get back into professional life on a case by case basis. The course meets for five days on two weekends beginning on Friday the first week and on Saturday morning the next. All classes start at 9:00 a.m. and last until 6:00 p.m.

I find a respite care agency that provides aides in order to give the caregiver a much-needed break. Since we are in the agency's catchment area, and we are not on Medicaid, we qualify for a limited number of hours, costs covered by the agency. New York really wants to help people age in place. Aging in place means that a person should be able to live out his or her life in his or her own apartment without having to move anywhere else.

I enroll to take the mediation course, pay the fee and buy the textbooks. The home health agency suggests that we have the aide visit us for several days prior to the time I'll be attending the course, so Bob and he can get to know each other.

"Fine," I say.

It's a Friday morning. I open the door to greet Barry. He is a sturdily-built Jamaican man in his forties, of average height, with a bright smile and a quiet voice.

"Good morning, ma'am," he begins, "My name is Barry from the Helping Angels Agency. You were expecting me?"

He has that lovely lilt in his voice which rises at the end of each sentence, even when it is not a question. He enters the apartment and stands in the middle of the living room, waiting. I offer him a seat, which he is reluctant to take, but I don't want Bob to feel intimidated by Barry's size.

"Barry," I say, "Please sit while I tell Bob that you are here." Barry sits and I go into Bob's room to invite him to join us.

"Bob, Barry is here. He wants to meet you," I explain to Bob, who walks out into the living room, takes one look at Barry and pulls me into our bedroom.

"Tell him to leave." He is agitated. "Tell him you made a mistake. Get him out of here." Bob is pushing me to leave the bedroom and speak to Barry. I try soothing him.

"Barry is only here to meet you. Next time he comes, he will take you to the doctor's office, as I have a conflicting appointment."

Bob comes out into the living room, "I don't need a babysitter," he tells Barry, "I can still wash and dress myself, can still make my own lunch and I don't need any help from you."

Barry is cordial enough, but understandably wary. He shakes Bob's hand, invites him to go for coffee so they can get to know each other a little bit. Bob turns him down, but agrees to go with Barry to the doctor's visit next time. Barry leaves.

I am not at home when Barry arrives on the day of the doctor's appointment. He takes Bob to the doctor, they go for doughnuts and coffee, and I am home when they return.

"Phyllis, can I see you in the other room for a minute?" Bob asks.

"Barry is still here," I say. "If this is about him and your time together, I think he should hear what you have to say." I am taking a risk here and I know it, but I think that openness is called for. Still, I am expecting a tirade.

"No," Bob says, "Barry did a WONDERFUL job. I was going to ask you for a check for one hundred dollars. I want to give Barry some money for taking me today, where you should have been taking me."

He's happy with Barry (unhappy with me). Barry smiles broadly, thanks Bob for the offer of payment and tells him the agency will take care of his pay.

It's now the following Friday, the first day of my course. I leave at 8:15 to be on site at a hotel by 9. Barry arrives at 8 a.m. Bob is asleep. I tell Barry to sit and read, until Bob wakes up. I've left his breakfast and a note telling Bob where I am, what time I will be home and a reminder to take his medications which are on the table, Bob needs no help with any tasks of daily living.

"Just hang loose," I tell him. I leave. I hear nothing all morning. At the noon break, I phone home.

"Everything is quiet," Barry tells me, but Bob doesn't want to go out for lunch as planned. He is making himself an omelet.

"Fine," I say.

At two o'clock there is a message on my phone. "Hello, this is Barry; your husband doesn't want me to stay. He became very angry with me and ordered me to leave – right away. I phoned my supervisor for instructions and she said it was all right for me to leave, so I left."

I phone home. I phone Barry. No one returns my calls. I leave the course an hour early, rushing back to our apartment. Bob is not home. He doesn't answer his

140

cell phone. I am frantic. There Is a note: "I went for a walk by myself."

But where could he have gone? Why is he not home yet? He walks in the door at 7 p.m. and says nothing.

I still have two more days of classes and cannot leave Bob alone. I appeal to my friends for help.

On Saturday, my friend Adele arrives at one o'clock. She invites Bob to go with her to the movies. He consents. She waits for him to shower and dress, and they go to the movies and back to Adele's apartment where I will join them. After I arrive, we all go out for dinner. Another day has been managed successfully.

Sunday morning, Bob is home alone. I leave the hotel early at lunchtime, go home and prepare lunch and medications while Bob showers and dresses. I return to the hotel for the afternoon session which starts at two o'clock.

As planned, our friend Herbie visits at 3 p.m. and goes with Bob to a neighborhood restaurant at 6.

After class, I grab a cab, and pick up Sandy, Herbie's wife, and we join the men at the restaurant. Thank you, our super friends. I feel I have accomplished a miraculous feat, but the stress is overwhelming for me.

Frank – In New York

In June, I hire Frank because he is a friend of Larry. Frank lives in New York and is currently between jobs. He is in his fifties, has the confident air of a successful businessman with a smile in greeting that makes everyone feel at home. Larry has told Frank about Bob and so Frank is prepared. He designs outings that he knows Bob will enjoy. Frank keeps Bob company during the two remaining days of my course work. I am much less stressed. They use our guidebook, "Fifty Walks in New York" and visit the garment district where Bob buys thread and needles for his sewing machine, although he isn't using the sewing machine any longer. They visit the subway museum that Bob had seen many years ago and still enjoys.

Lyle – In New York

However, after a few weeks, Frank informs us he has taken a full time job. But he recommends a friend, Lyle, whom he is sure Bob will like. We have to start all over again. Lyle is a charming man in his fifties, bald with wisps of white hair, tall and dapper, with the easily burned skin of northern European ancestry. He has a kind face, a warm smile and a gentle demeanor. I'd like him to be my companion. He is so patient with Bob, but my husband's illness now causes him to be obstreperous.

Sometimes Bob refuses to go on an outing after Lyle arrives. Sometimes Bob refuses to go where Lyle has planned to take him. Bob complains to Lyle also, and Lyle listens patiently, but Bob's tone and his anger directed towards me are very hard to take.

Lyle has success taking Bob by bus to thrift stores and to watch the workers in the street constructing a new subway line. They travel by subway to Fourteenth Street to shop, to the 99 cent stores, to the Salvation Army store, to the Home Depot, but Bob's interest in these former happy pursuits decreases steadily and it becomes harder and harder to engage him in an activity.

Whenever I need coverage throughout the summer and early fall, Lyle is there. I can count on him. He even meets me at the hospital when I have cataract surgery and entertains Bob for the rest of the day so I can rest. When I awake, Bob has also been napping in his room, and Lyle is quietly reading in the living room.

By November, Bob is continually refusing to go with Lyle and the visits stop. Bob is not willing to go with me, either. He just wants to stay home.

Wally – In New York

Our friend Sandy informs me that her husband Herbie is not feeling well and will probably not be able to meet Bob for lunch one afternoon each week as he had last summer. So Sandy has inquired on our behalf and has found Wally, their neighbor, who has offered to be Bob's lunch companion once each week. I now have another option.

Wally is a recently retired stock broker who still follows the market on the computer and walks his dog religiously at 2:30 each afternoon. So he has a short window to have lunch with Bob. These visits work well for a short while, but then Bob complains that he does not need a babysitter in his neighborhood and he begins to refuse Wally's patient, calm offers to lunch.

Kathie and Zena – In Arizona

In New York, I have a woman who comes to clean our apartment. Over the course of time, Bob has gotten used to her and I can leave the house while Anna is cleaning. Bob will sometimes go for a walk by himself, but only in the neighborhood, and I am only away for a few hours. So I thought I would try to find a cleaning woman in Arizona. So far, I have hired a cleaning service; five women bring their own supplies and clean my house from top to bottom in an hour. But I need respite. I am willing to wait for Bob to develop a comfortable relationship with a woman whose job it will be to clean the house.

First, I hire a woman, Kathie, who advertises in the local newspaper. Her clothing smells from smoke. Bob looks at her and yells, "Where's Phyllis?" The gardener arrives and Kathie is abrupt with him. She is a capable house cleaner, but not a caregiver. I need a trained person to supervise my husband. But I have no respite, no ability to leave the house without my spouse.

Next, I call a home health agency. A woman asks to set up a home visit to discuss my needs; we decide that the agency will send a home health aide to clean once a week for four hours. I pay in advance. The woman they send, Zena, arrives once, but refuses to return, complaining to her supervisor that she had been trained to be a caregiver, not a cleaning woman. I still haven't found the answer. I need help and good trained help is hard to find.

19 – What is Selfish?

Bob is not in the living room, sitting in his favorite chair. He is not at the table where he reads his morning paper. There is no shower water running. He is not in the kitchen, eating ice cream from the carton. I see into our bedroom. He is not in bed. I enter the room we call Bob's Room. There he is, in his pajamas and terry cloth robe, blinds still drawn from last night, air conditioner off, lights off. He is seated on the futon, holding one of the decorative pillows to his chest.

"Hi Hon," I say. No response, but he looks at me.

"What's up?" Bob shrugs his shoulders.

"I just got back from the gym," I tell him. Bob looks at me and says, "I wanted to hold you but you weren't here, so I'm hugging the pillow instead." I go over and give him a hug. But he just sits there, lumpy. The moment has passed. I cannot make it better.

This illness is so unfair. We had cuddle time this morning. Bob had a nice long backrub. He murmured, "You don't know how good it feels to hold you," a few hours ago. The memory is gone. Sometime while I was at the gym, he woke up and I was not there to fulfill his immediate wish. This stopped him in his tracks. He used the bathroom, put on his robe and has just been sitting here, bereft, a bit angry even, until now.

I understand now so much better what my mother was experiencing when she complained that I didn't visit or call, when I had been to see her. Or when she complained to me that my sister Sharyn hadn't been there. "It's the NOW, stupid," could be the political cry of Alzheimer's disease.

When Lyle comes to take him for an outing, Bob is still in the shower. When I knock to remind Bob that Lyle is here, Bob says, "I thought he was coming at 1:30. I'll be ready in twenty minutes." *How come now, he knows the time and can estimate it as well?*

So Lyle and I talk and wait. Bob comes out all spiffy and shiny, shaved, dressed and smiling. Smiles are infrequent these days. "Wow, you look nice," I smile back at him.

Another smile. "What's so funny?"

I seem never to know when to just stay quiet.

Bob responds, "I'm smiling because you are such a shmuck."

"Oops, time to go to Home Depot with Lyle," I quickly respond. *Bob has never used that kind of language.* But if I draw attention to it, I will not get free time and the outing will suffer. So now I know to keep still. "Lyle needs your help finding a drill bit for his drill."

They leave. Later, Lyle reports back that he saw no negativity during the afternoon, and as soon as they were in the elevator, Bob turned to him and said, "I don't know why I said that to Phyllis."

Last night, I was on the phone with my son Steve. Bob asked to speak with him. He took the telephone into his room and closed the door. Steve emailed me later to tell me what had happened. They talked about the house in Arizona that Steve checks on for us. Steve

146

spoke of a tree in the front that my son-in-law Dave had trimmed. Bob had trouble visualizing the tree and told Steve we'll be coming to Arizona soon.

Then he said, "Your mother is terrible to me. She is never home. And when she is home, she is always on the computer." Steve said he asked if Bob is often home alone. "No," Bob responded, "I am not alone."

My feelings fluctuate wildly. This illness is so unpredictable. One minute I am the best wife there is, the next minute I am a selfish person, wanting to escape any way I can. In actuality, I structure my time now to be at the gym four mornings a week, away from home for two hours. I have arranged to have two afternoons a week to myself, for four hours each. This week and again in two weeks I have been invited to the theater without Bob. I also have tickets with Bob to Avery Fisher Hall. Every summer Lincoln Center for the Arts sponsors a series of concerts featuring Bob's favorite composer, Mozart. As we drove by Lincoln Center on the bus, Bob saw the large banner advertising the concerts and said he wanted to see and hear the first "Mostly Mozart" concert. He asked me to get tickets for our friends and for us. I bought less expensive tickets than before, so if Bob wants to leave at intermission, I will not be as upset. Last time we were at Avery Fisher Hall, Bob was tired of "too much music" after the first Beethoven symphony. So we will see. I also have purchased two tickets to "Come Fly Away" a musical play on Broadway, for Bob's birthday. He loves Frank Sinatra and Twyla Tharp. We loved "Movin' Out". I expect he will enjoy the experience while we are there.

Last summer in New York, 2009, we had many out of town guests. Each set wanted to go to the theater. So we saw "Billie Elliot", "Shrek", "Desire under the Elms," "Xanadu" and "Mary Stuart." Bob sat between our two grandsons and enjoyed them watching "Shrek". He enjoyed sitting with his granddaughter Sara watching the dancing Billie Elliot and loved the steamy scenes in "Desire under the Elms", although he mumbled to me that "this was taking too long." The only one he actually walked out on was Mary Stuart. He couldn't hear it well; we were seated under the overhang in the orchestra. There was a lot of talking and not much action.

"I am not staying. I am going home by myself. I will take the subway." He is adamant. I am embarrassed. We are with another couple, Amy and Dominick. Amy is one of my dearest friends, but her husband has not seen Bob since this illness descended upon us. I follow Bob to the lobby at intermission with the smokers.

"Bob, I will agree for you to go home by yourself, but let's find a cab," I say as I show my ticket stub to the usher. He agrees I can go out and return. As we exit the theater, Bob looks up.

"There's the restaurant we had lunch in last time. I can go in there, have coffee and a dessert and meet you out here when the play is over." Great idea that works out well.

Now a year later, Bob is in a different place. I will leave him home alone this Saturday night while I attend a performance of "The Merchant of Venice" in Central Park with my neighbor, Eileen. The performance begins at eight. But on August third, I have asked his niece

Jeannie to have dinner with Bob at home without me, as I will leave at 6:00 to meet Amy for a snack and a 7:30 curtain of "Our Town." I don't know how any of these plans will work.

20 – Psychotic Break in Arizona

Arizona, May 2010

It's the end of May. My grandson Austin is about to graduate from high school. Bob and I will return to Arizona for the event. But first I must make plans. While I'd like Bob to join us at the graduation, I don't want to have to worry about him – about whether he'd insist we leave during the proceedings, for example. I'd like everyone's attention to be focused on the graduate. I need someone who will be with Bob, whether at the ceremony or at home. I ask Bob's brother Irving, to accompany us and he agrees. I enjoy Irving's company and appreciate his help.

Irving is 87 years young. He is mentally agile, but has encountered some physical problems of late. Not too long ago, he was walking in a parking lot when he was hit by a car driven by a fellow octogenarian. He suffered a broken ankle and does not feel confident about traveling alone. And so I make plans. Bob and I fly from New York to Atlanta. Irving flies to Atlanta from Florida. We meet and then all three fly to Arizona together, where we are met at the airport by my son, Steve.

It's a good thing Irving is able to accompany us as Bob becomes cantankerous on graduation day. I am not surprised. I know I just changed the structure of Bob's life. People with Alzheimer's disease have a hard time dealing with change and we just flew from one home to another in a different part of the country. Bob is disturbed and he lets me know it. Bob does not want to attend the graduation, "You are making such a fuss over a high school graduation," he complains. "It might mean something if it were a college graduation." When I tell him that both he and Irving have been invited to the family party and the graduation ceremony, he yells, "What business would my brother have going there? It's too long to sit around, and too hot. We'll stay right here."

And they do, although I wish they could be there for the 7 o'clock ceremony. The sunset is gorgeous, with the sky turning orange and pink, then purple, as a backdrop to the lush green of the field, the colorful robes of the faculty and students and the bright uniforms of the school band.

During the next two days, Steve chauffeurs Irving and Bob to an ammunition supply store in Scottsdale and takes them to a shooting range. Irving loves guns and Steve is determined that Irving have some fun while he's here. What happens next is a horrendous example of how anyone's best plans can go astray when you are dealing with the worst of illnesses. On Sunday afternoon, Steve arrives after a swim and walks into the room where Bob and Irving are having a conversation. He invites them out for dinner at a Chinese restaurant, a last meal before Irving leaves for Florida the next morning. Steve smiles at the two men. "The treat's on me," he says.

"With you looking like that?" Bob counters with a mean look on his face. "I wouldn't go anywhere with you looking like that. You haven't shaved. You're wearing ratty clothing. No, no, NO."

We are dumbfounded. I am seated at the dining table. Steve walks toward me and sits down. Bob follows, standing. He begins to rant about me and my children. Irving meanwhile has retreated to the guest bedroom, embarrassed.

"Ok., we don't have to go," I say. "Steve was only trying to be nice." I try to agree with Bob, but the mention of Steve sets him off again. "Always about you and your children. I don't know what to do about you. I feel like..." and he picks up a silver bowl from the counter, raising his arm as if to hit me. Steve stands up. I stand, face Steve and tell him to sit back down.

Bob is still screaming. "What can I destroy to make you understand?" He walks toward the front of the house, where there is an antique chest we had brought with us from New York. This chest had been shipped from Germany by my grandparents in 1923. Now Bob is screaming, "This chest is important to you. I'm going to break it; I need to do something to show you so you know how mad I am." He raises the silver bowl and is about to smash it against the chest. I come up behind him and take his arm, grabbing the bowl from him. He pulls his arm free, relinquishing the bowl.

"Bob, calm down," I say firmly. "Get yourself in control. Don't try to hit me, or I will have to call 911."

Bob swivels and enters my office, slamming the glass doors so that they rattle. "I'll show you," he screams. He then knocks over a bookcase, scattering my professional hardcover books on the floor. He picks up one book at random, "Play Therapy with Children in Crisis", and tears pages from the book, throwing the pages down and glaring at me. I stand paralyzed, mesmerized by the sight of him so enraged. He then takes the cover of the book with its remaining pages and begins smashing my laptop with it, successfully destroying the hard drive. I come to my senses and dial 911. I see that Irving is standing, watching this melee, face reddened, hands clenched. I am afraid he'll have a stroke.

"Irv, it's okay." I put my arm around him. "We'll get the police officer to get Bob to take some of his medicine, and he will calm down."

"That's not my brother. That's not my brother. My brother doesn't act like that. Never in my whole life have I seen my brother angry." Irving is crying. Bob is sitting in my desk chair, watching us.

"Did you call the police?" Bob asks me, belligerently.

"Yes, I did," I answer quietly. "They will be here soon." The dispatcher keeps me on the phone until the police arrive.

"What did you tell them, that I'm the one that's crazy?" Bob is ready to start up again. Irving opens the door, pulls up a chair and sits next to his brother. We all wait for the police.

What do I expect the police to do? I expect them to interview my husband, get him to take his medicine and evaluate if they feel he needs to be hospitalized or taken for a psychiatric evaluation. Two young police officers arrive, dressed in full uniform with holstered weapons. They walk into the house, see Bob in my office with his brother and follow me into the kitchen area.

"Did he hit you?" one of the policemen asks. It is his first question.

"No," I respond, "but..."

"Because the law states that if he hit you, that's domestic violence and we have to take him in."

"Take him in where?" I ask naively.

"To jail. And since it is Sunday, he probably would have to spend the night and be arraigned in the morning. But," he hesitates, "that probably wouldn't do you much good if he already has a diagnosis."

My head is swimming. What is this man saying? When will he interview my husband? When will he ask what happened? He is sort of talking out loud to himself, figuring things out.

"Sir," I begin, "We are generally winter residents here. We live in New York the rest of the year. So I am not familiar with your regulations. Please explain to me your procedures for calming a demented person. Did I make a mistake calling 911?"

"No ma'am. That's what we're here for. To protect you from domestic violence. I'm just saying, it doesn't look like it would do you much good to have this man thrown in jail overnight."

"Could you get him to take his medicine?" I ask.

"No, we can't do that. How do we know what medicine he needs?" he replies obliquely.

"Could you take him to the hospital?" I ask again.

"No, we're only permitted to escort him to jail," he answers factually.

"Can you go in and talk to him; perhaps ask his brother to give him his medications?" I try once more.

154

"Sure, we'd be happy to talk with him. If his brother gives him the medicine, we won't interfere."

Okay. I get two 25 mg Seroquel tablets and a glass of water; bring them with me and the two officers to the door of my office. I hand the pills and the water to Irving. I don't look at Bob.

"Irv, would you please give these two pills to Bob? They will help him to calm down," I say as I leave the room. Steve and I sit at the table. Steve is all shaken up. He is so upset. "I thought he was going to hit you," he says. "I couldn't let him hit you. And you stopped me. Why did you stop me? I wasn't the one trying to hurt anyone." Steve thinks I blame him.

"Son, you did nothing wrong. I just needed to protect you both. You listened. Bob didn't. He wasn't able to control himself. I was shocked, but I didn't think he could hurt me. I know I was sitting and he was standing. I know how it looked. He is a sick man. We all have to realize that." I hope Steve understands and that he does not take the insults personally.

Soon, the police officers return to the kitchen. Since someone (Irving) is with Bob they say it might be a good time for Steve and me to leave for a while, at least until the medication takes effect and Bob calms down or goes to sleep. They advise me to call again if my husband hits me, and they will press charges.

Steve and I go to Linda's, where we are grateful for some peace and quiet. A few hours later, I return home. Bob is asleep on the living room couch. Irv is watching the television news. The next morning, I drive Irving to the airport. Bob is still asleep on the couch.

21 – Avon-by-the-Sea

New York, July 2010

I am forever making mistakes. Take this week for example. It is July, a steaming hot day in New York City, so hot that someone actually tried to fry an egg on the street. It didn't work because he used a frying pan. Had he just cracked an egg on the asphalt, I am sure it would have fried. Even so, believe me, it is hot and the humidity makes the air thick. The hot weather makes everyone think of the beach, especially me. My family and I spent every summer near the ocean when I was a child growing up in New Jersey. The weather reports every day feature ocean temps, sunburn advisories and traffic reports. I yearn to see the ocean. I start remembering my favorite beach mini-vacations.

Bob and I have been going to the same inn at Avon-by-the-Sea, to a historic Victorian seaside resort in Monmouth County, New Jersey for twenty years. Before our marriage, I vacationed there as a single. In those days, the inn was run by an elderly German woman who set rules; no men allowed in the rooms of single women guests, breakfast served at a specific time and no later, wet bathing suits to be hung outside on the line. The inn, although a bit shabby is situated one street from the boardwalk and from my favorite room, number fifteen on the third floor, I can see a sliver of ocean. The room faces east; there is a large restaurant on the corner which only partially blocks my view, the garbage trucks sometimes interrupt my sleep, as they pick up the trash and especially the glass bottles very early in the morning. The north and east facing windows offer a cool ocean breeze. I love it. The floor has four bathrooms in a row on the northern side. "My" room is right next to one of them, which is another reason it's my favorite room. I love the wicker chair with the flowered cushion and the old time chenille bedspread on the double bed.

One day, I am surprised to meet a patient of mine, seated on the porch. "Hello, Dr. Palm," says the young woman. "What a super surprise to see you. Sam, come and see who is here. This is my doctor. I told you so much about her."

I'm embarrassed. It can be uncomfortable to see a patient in another setting. I smile and greet her. The innkeeper is her aunt. But I now receive preferred treatment from the innkeeper. So of course, I want to share with Bob the pleasure of my special retreat.

In 1992, a terrible storm causes a great deal of damage to the area. When we arrive the following summer, we find the ownership changed and the Inn refurbished. Bob and I are assigned to room fifteen as I requested, but it is now renamed the Wisteria Room. An AC unit shutters the north facing window. The nearby bath has been incorporated into the room. There are new curtains and the wallpaper has been changed, but the comfy double bed with the chenille coverlet is still there. So is the wicker chair. We like the new owners, Bill and Kathy and especially their black lab, Maggie. Bob visits the annual Ocean Grove town-wide flea market the weekend after Labor Day in the neighboring quaint Victorian era town. My place becomes "our" special sanctuary. We are both very happy.

We spend many long weekends at the inn. Bill is recuperating from heart surgery and works now from home, but we don't know when they retire and sell the inn. New owners greet us once again. We soon discover that the new owner, also named Bob, had been in the US Army, a company clerk as my husband had been many years before. The two men spend hours talking army talk, enjoying each other's company. The owner is a fisherman as well as an innkeeper. He catches "stripers" large striped bass, on a rod from the beach, entering his catch in local contests. One day he shows us a 42 inch striper in a cooler on ice in the backyard. When we leave for home, he hands us two large slices of striper. "See you next year," he says as we wave goodbye from our car.

Last summer, many weekends were rainy and we didn't go overnight to the beach. Instead, our friends Sandy and Herbie drove us to Long Beach, a rustic town on Long Island, for a day trip. We enjoyed a walk on the large, wide boardwalk, smelled the fresh sea air and enjoyed a seafood dinner in one of the many Italian eateries on the main street.

This year, when I ask Bob to go with me to the inn, he refuses. "I don't feel safe." he says. He remembers the generosity of the owner and he remembers the fish, but it is not enough to lure him back. Bob doesn't want to go to the beach, "too much sand." He doesn't want to take the train, "takes too long." He doesn't want to go to the flea market, "We have no more room to put stuff."

So what is my mistake? When life is going smoothly, I let my expectations increase, only to have them knocked down again. I am told repeatedly by Marilynn and other spouses whose loved ones have dementia to "reduce your expectations to zero" in order to avoid the deflated feeling I have now. It's a hot day; I am thinking how nice it would be to plan a weekend at the beach. It doesn't have to be today, but before the season is over. It doesn't have to be Avon, I'll settle for a day boat trip to Sandy Hook, or even a walk on the boardwalk at Coney Island. Not to be. A whole day away from my husband is too long. He becomes agitated if I am not within reach for more than a few hours. A substitute caregiver may sometimes take over for four hours at most. Further, Bob cannot venture far from home base, even with me by his side. All change can be so disruptive. Life is so frightening when you cannot remember, cannot predict even the near future and feel so insecure.

22 – Social Misbehaviors

New York, September 2010

"Do you know those are my cars?" Bob asks as he walks into the living room from his room.

"Yep, sure do. Elijah is enjoying playing with them. See how he's got them all lined up at the edge of the buffet, ready to go?" I answer cheerfully, as I watch my almost three year old great nephew play on the floor.

"Would you mind if I picked them up and put them back in the bag?" asks Bob.

Oh my. Elijah looks crestfallen. He says to his mommy, "I think I'd like to clean them up now," and he places the cars in their bag and hands the bag to Bob.

This is a collection of Matchbox cars, without boxes and not in pristine condition. There's a Corgi London taxi, and a small, wooden toy car as well. Bob cannot be concerned about their collectible value. They are not Antiques Road-Show material. I am so surprised at my husband and so upset that Elijah feels he has done something wrong.

"Bob," I explain, "This is my sister Rita's son, Aaron, his wife Rachel, Elijah and his baby brother Levi. They are visiting the city from California for two weeks and we have just returned from the American Museum of Natural History." Bob did not say hello to them. He does not remember them, although we attended their wedding, and they were our guests for a week when they visited New York when Elijah was five months old. When we walked in earlier, Bob just looked out from the kitchen where he was drying a dish.

"We're going to have some lunch. Will you have a bowl of soup with us?" I ask as I walk into the narrow kitchen, giving him a hug as I pass by on my way to the fridge.

"I just ate. Why are you going to mess up the kitchen? I just cleaned it." Bob sounds exasperated.

"We just got back and we're hungry. Rachel gave the boys some snacks, but we're going to have some bagels and cream cheese and lox. I'm getting everything out now. First, some iced coffee. We're thirsty." I talk as I take out the food. I really wish I had some notice that they were coming today. I would have prepared something, but in the rain, it is impossible. We'll make do with what's here.

Bob goes from the kitchen into his room, without saying hello or playing with the sweet little boys. It's so weird. On the street, he stops every stroller to play hide and seek with the child.

"I already ate. Why are you going to mess up the kitchen? I just cleaned it," Bob repeats, clearly in a mood. I prepare lunch and Bob retreats into his room.

Sometimes he is like that when guests come for dinner, too. When Adele walks into the apartment, she often asks, "What's he like today? Is it a good day or a bad day? Should I I say hello to him or not?"

I always answer, "Sure, say hello. It is so unpredictable. He may be fine." And sometimes he is. Other times he says, "Why are you eating here again?" *Does this illness give him the right to be downright rude to guests?*

We are invited to a party at which the hosts pour glasses of champagne to make a toast. Some filled glasses are on the table, waiting to be served. Bob goes up to the table, picks up a glass, sees that it is not full, pours some champagne into it from another poured glass, and drinks it. He trips someone on his way to the table, doesn't notice. He sees something he wants and goes for it. I apologize to the woman he tripped. She smiles and says, "We all know. It's all right."

This is the same man who asked me yesterday, "What is Alzheimer's?" He was reading the NY Times and the headline stated that a new protein has been discovered that will aid in the development of new medications to slow the progress of this disease. I think he just read the headline.

"Alzheimer's is a disease that makes lots of people lose their memories. There is a lot of research going on now to find a cure for it." I say, diplomatically.

"I don't have it," Bob says.

"What do you have?" I ask knowing it's the wrong thing to say.

"There is nothing wrong with me. You are just making stuff up so I will die and you can have my money."

In for a nickel, in for a dime. I continue.

"Do you remember the day we went on an airplane and you felt dizzy?"

"Yes, they came with a wheelbarrow to get me off the plane."

"Right, and Doctor A. told you that one medicine didn't go with some others you were taking?"

162

"Right and I made the right decision there, too. I wasn't going back there. She should have known better," he says.

"Well, that was the first time you were diagnosed with Alzheimer-like memory loss. I remember you got real mad when Dr. A. wrote on the lab referral, under reason for referral, 'Dementia'. Dementia is another way of describing the same thing. That was in 2006. It is four years later now."

Bob is very quiet. He goes into his den, sits on his couch and falls asleep. The next day I find a magazine in his room called "The Bottom Line, Health," open to the page "Answer found to Alzheimer's Disease" advertising a book called "Ultimate Healing." It suggests supplements to take and dietary changes to "reverse the aging process." So far, he hasn't shown me the magazine. I hope he hasn't ordered the book because the tools in the book are directed at people who have normal aging questions, poor eating habits perhaps, are smokers, or drinkers, and need to alter their behavior to avoid developing neurological problems as far as behavioral changes allow. They are not for diagnosed cases of dementia.

23 – Happy Birthday

New York, July 2010

It is early morning, well not that early. I leave the house at 8:41. As it is not a gym day, I decide to go for a walk in Central Park. But first I stop off at the post office to mail a package that Bob was to have sent off earlier... only he forgot to buy the stamps. Luckily, there is no line at the post office. I then enter the park, pass the Delacorte Theater, visit the turtles in their pond, and walk around the Great lawn to the east where the tall trees still shade the path. I walk through the Pinetum where the tall evergreens provide shade all day. I am still accompanied only by a few dog walkers or exercisers like myself. I arrive at the Reservoir and pick up my pace traveling east, then north, in the shade. As I turn west, along the north rim of the water, I hear a goose honking noisily. There is a gander on the running path, assuredly searching for an opening to enter the reservoir.

More honking. The goose, followed closely by an adolescent gosling, is walking in a wire mesh fenced-in enclosure a short distance away. I imagine their conversation from the tone of their voices:

She: "Come this way. You'll never find an opening there."

He: "Sure I will. There are other geese in the water. Don't you hear them? I want to get into the water, too."

She: "Walk this way with me. There is an open field. You can get a head start. You know junior can't fly over

164

that fence without a head start." They keep honking, responsively. He keeps preening. She is steadily walking east with their gosling following her quietly, nibbling at the new grass seeds as he walks.

I am surrounded by the ganders of this world. They are all off doing their thing, successfully or not, but not at all concerned that I must follow the treaded path, dutifully taking care. I can steal away for an hour in the morning, while Bob is still asleep. As long as I remember to put out his medications, and his breakfast and a note, detailing what he must do and in which order, where I am and when I will return, it will be all right, I hope.

It will be my husband's 81st birthday on Friday. He's not seen any of his children since April 10. That was three months ago. Nor have they phoned to make a plan to visit him for his birthday, not even the one who lives an hour away in New Jersey.

My brood is no better. They phone when they need something from me, not to listen, offer support or cheer or even a funny story. My daughter and her family are flying to New Jersey today. They will stay at my sister's family beach house for the week. They will not come to visit me. We are not welcome there. My sister does not speak to me, but she lures my daughter with tickets and the ocean.

No matter. We will still celebrate Bob's birthday. When his meds are working, my husband still enjoys getting dressed nicely and eating in a fine restaurant. Our friends, Sandy and Herbie, phone and ask us to join them for dinner in honor of Sandy's birthday and Bob's. What a nice idea. What great friends they are. We make a 6:30 reservation at La Mirabelle, an old traditional Upper West Side French restaurant right across the street from our apartment. Even a sudden thunderstorm will not stop us.

Tonight, Bob is calm. He looks around him appreciatively. Our friends have arrived before us; they welcome us to the table. The waitress opens the menus, and places one in each of our hands. We peruse the menus. She returns and lists the specials. She is standing next to my husband, so she is not looking at him. He touches the pad that the specials are written on, in an attempt to see what she is saying. She leaves.

After a few minutes, we are all talking about what we will order. My husband turns to me and says sadly, "I don't even know the names of the foods anymore." I suggest the Cornish game hen, preceded by the potato and leek vichyssoise. He shrugs, agreeing to the hen, but not wanting cold soup. We decide to share a salad with goat cheese, and he loves it.

"It's arugula, I think," he says happily. He is right. I order a *Muscadet,* a Loire valley wine, which helps us all enjoy the meal and the camaraderie. Whenever Sandy or Herbie ask a question, Bob's response is way off. For example, they ask us about our Restaurant Week lunch the week before. Bob doesn't remember any of it. I tell them about our meal and the setting.

Herbie asks, "What happened Friday on the bus? Did you fall? Did someone push you?"

"I don't like cold soup." Bob answers.

They shrug and continue the conversation as if he isn't with us. I feel awful. I feel torn as well. I want to

166

participate with them, discussing upcoming trips they will take, yet I feel Bob is abandoned. I reach out to hold his hand, trying to establish contact physically, as our friends are speaking. But now, he pushes my hand away. "What's the matter?" he asks.

Just like last week, the day of the Terrace in the Sky restaurant lunch. I want to sit on the bus next to Marilynn, who accompanied us, so I don't sit with Bob in the front of the bus, as I usually do. As I walk to the rear, Bob follows me, falls and now he has this gash on his shin which is so noticeable because it is summer and he wears shorts.

The next week, Sandy and Herbie invite me to join them to see a foreign language film on a day that Bob has a hired companion to be with him. I enjoy the afternoon, but I miss Bob, as it is usually the four of us together, not only three. Herbie calls me the next day. "I think you made the right choice, not bringing Bob to see this foreign film," he says. "He would not have understood it." Herbie, too, is feeling torn, between including and abandoning his friend. *Of course I am feeling guilty. Am I now like the gander, off doing my own thing at the expense of my demented spouse?*

24 – Emotional Bank Account

New York, September 2010

I take very seriously the admonition that we care-givers must take care of ourselves so that we can better manage the physical and emotional demands involved in caring for a loved one. That's the reason I go to the gym, and walk three miles a day. In addition, I have some digestive issues and maintain a dairy-free and gluten-free regimen (plus probiotics) to deal with them. When Bob starts to toss and turn and to get up and walk about at irregular hours, I replace our queen-sized mattress with two single mattresses hoping that would help me get some much needed rest (that part isn't working yet). The point is I'm following all the advice on how to maintain my health and energy; eat right, get a good night's rest, exercise. There is one more element of course, reduce stress.

Is that why I have less energy than before? Why I have less stamina, less flexibility, less strength, than I had a few years ago? Gary Chapman in his book, "The Five Love Languages" explains that all relationships are based on each partner feeling loved, and that we each experience that feeling differently. Some of us appreciate tasks accomplished for us as the other person's way of showing love. Some of us feel loved when we receive a card or flowers or chocolates. Some feel loved when our partner talks to us and listens attentively to what we say. And some feel loved especially when we are physically touched. Balancing the feelings of both partners in a relationship often ends the friction that would bring couples into my office for counseling.

I would see this often in couples who came to my office on the brink of divorce. One partner would complain that her spouse had plenty of energy for golf, but not for sex. Another partner might complain that his wife didn't appreciate his completing all the "honey-do" projects she handed him, which took up all of his free time. Or one would be hurt because the other didn't make an effort to be home in time to eat the meal that was especially prepared, or to think to purchase flowers for a special event. Each of these partners felt he or she was working hard at providing what was needed to sustain the family, each was stressed and disappointed in the relationship, while not knowing what it was that the partner needed in order to feel loved.

Until the illness began, my husband had shown me love in all those ways. I was blessed with a second marriage in which we both knew the importance of working on our relationship. We were also at a point in our lives when outside pressures were reduced so we could concentrate on loving each other. All of our children were grown and out of the house. Our combined earnings afforded us a comfortable life style. I "banked" all of those good feelings in my personal self-worth account. Even as my husband loses his ability to do household chores, for example, I remember the ones he did routinely without being asked. We shared many tasks, and frankly, once he retired, he did more of them than I. He still can clean up the kitchen after a meal better than I can, but he does need a reminder, and he lets me know that he feels burdened by my request. I still ask him, however, because it's good for him to be and feel useful. When a task like chopping the vegetables for salad is done, he can point to his accomplishment and say, "Didn't I do a good job making salad?"

Bob also folds the clothes after they are washed and dried. We made a pact when we were first married that he doesn't decide what goes into the washer or the dryer. I lost a few nice pieces that way. So I leave the clean clothes basket on the bed, and wait until he decides to fold them. Monitoring this task helps me gauge the changes in Bob's ability as well. I can see where I am needed and what he can still handle. Usually Bob places his clothes in his drawers, and leaves my folded clothing on the bed. This week I note that he is unable to keep my white undergarments separate from his. Anything white goes into his drawer. Nor can he sort white socks with differing patterns. All white socks get folded together, and end up in his sock drawer, too.

Life cycle events are an area Bob has trouble remembering. When Bob stopped sending his children cards and checks for their birthdays, he also stopped recognizing my birthday or our anniversary, but I try to arrange something festive for those special days. I may even treat myself to some small item, tell him it's his gift to me and thank him for it. He still says, "Anything you want. You know I don't want to deprive you of anything." This way we both feel good. I've also learned to share my special day with others. Bringing a cake to a religious group meeting or to a support group meeting and celebrating with friends helps me keep a positive outlook and satisfies somewhat my need to feel loved through receiving and giving something of value.

It is hard to preserve the special nature of a relationship in the best of times, and now it is much more difficult as previously tendered acts of affection turn into obligation. The other day Bob woke up next to me, looked at me and said, "The best part of every day is waking up next to you." That touched me so deeply. I have loved waking up next to him for so many years. But the following scenario is much more typical lately.

It's morning. He wakes me up at 5:21 a.m., wanting a hug. I am not pleasant, rolling him over and as nicely as I can, say, "It's very early. Go back to sleep." At 7 o'clock on the dot, I feel him petting me once again. I feel like a blow-up doll, providing a place for him to express his physical needs. It is not me, his loving wife that he is feeling affection for. Perhaps I "should" like it, but I don't. And as a therapist and a friend I preach always that "should" is a magic word. It lets the person who says it know that the action is not something he or she wants to do, but somehow feels obliged to do. Here are some other examples of "shoulds":

"I should go visit my mother today." "I should pay those bills before I go out." "I should not eat that piece of cake."

I have been fortunate. I have my own life, my own work, I have not been dependent on my spouse for all the love in my life and I have over the last 20 years received a lot of love. But a demented spouse, whether from Parkinson's disease, Alzheimer's disease or other causes loses the ability to provide love in any of the ways Chapman details, and the balance in that joint bank account shifts. It is a slow change, and one that can go unrecognized by the caregiver for a while, and it takes its toll. I believe this reduction in transmitting loving feelings causes a decline in the caregiver. It is why, despite my self-care, I feel less energetic, less vital as time goes by. Physical as well as psychological damage occurs. That is what I am feeling now.

25 – Just like in Morocco

New York, August 2010

Anyone seeing Marilynn and me on this day might think we were two women without a care between us. In fact, we are two tired women, both of us caregiving spouses who have decided a break in routine is not just recommended, it is essential. I tell you about this day in the hope that if you are involved in caring for someone, you'll be encouraged to give yourself a break.

We are without our husbands, wearing jeans and sandals with our diamond wedding and engagement rings. We take the subway downtown to Canal Street. We enjoy the ride, as itinerant musicians entertain us with their music, sung by three guitarists and a bass. Climbing the stairs with an extra lilt to our steps, we arrive to see the sun shining from behind the white clouds. What sky we can see is the blue of August. Several streets radiate like spokes around a myriad of traffic signs. Heading toward the sun, remaining on the same street, my friend delightedly announces, "I recognize where we are. It's just like in Morocco. See that shop?"

Walking toward the small storefront, we enter and see souvenir items. We browse like tourists from store to store. I see nothing of interest to me. An Asian woman on the street wearing a light green cardigan sweater approaches, "Handbags? Ladies' Rolex watches? Tiffany jewelry?"

I nod my head. She crooks her finger in the universal sign which means 'follow me'.

Marilynn whispers, "Are you sure you want to do this?"

We follow as the woman takes quick, small, furtive steps. She turns the corner. We see another small store, only this one has a door, not a metal roll down as the others have. She motions for us to enter as she remains outside, cell phone to her ear. I imagine she is telling someone, "We've got a hot one here."

The door closes behind us. There are scarves, jewelry, a counter but no handbags. We wait. As a woman comes slowly out from behind the counter, she pockets the cell phone that has just beeped.

"Handbags?" she asks.

I nod. She turns away from us, opening a concealed panel door to the right, behind the counter, listening for some sound that would prevent her movement. The woman motions for us to descend a narrow flight of cement steps. She follows, closing the door behind her. When we reach the cellar, she makes a phone call and leaves. *Will we be okay down here*? Another door opens. A man is bending over a large box as he unpacks handbags with designer labels. He pays no attention to us as we shop. *He must have opened the door. No one else is here, right*? I see a bag I like. He then begins to talk, explaining that this bag is one of the newest ones for the coming season. He has been listening intently to our conversation. My friend does not see a bag with a shoulder strap. Well, actually she does like the same one I have my eye on, but with a long strap. I can tell we

174

don't want to purchase the same bag. I bargain, but he will not reduce the price far enough. We leave. I think if we both see a bag we like, we will have more bargaining power.

We continue to walk up the stairs. The seller calls out a lower price. I say no. He lowers the price once more. I should have acquiesced, but I don't. I feel funny. This is not legal. At the least, they deprive the government of tax money. These bags are knockoffs. I haven't done comparison shopping. I don't know what the true value of the handbag is. We leave. We walk further up the street, browsing in similar storefronts to the first. Some sell perfume. I am thinking about the secrecy and the hiding from the police. I am feeling a bit uncomfortable, but also a bit excited. A man walks next to us this time.

"Ladies Rolex?" he whispers. My friend says, "I already have one." I elbow her to be quiet.

"What are you looking for? Handbags? I have Gucci, Coach, and Chanel."

"Yes, but the price has to be right." I say.

"How many pieces?" he asks, as we continue to walk side by side down the block.

"Two," I answer.

"What price?" I tell him my low price.

"That's too little money. These bags go for twice that," he says.

"Forget it then. I don't need a handbag that is so expensive."

"But uptown, the price is much higher." I shrug my shoulders and walk on. He catches up to me.

175

"Okay. I give you special morning price. Two bags, your price. Follow me. We have to be very careful," he says in a stage whisper. *Who is fooling whom? We don't look like residents of this community. If the police are watching, of course they see what we are doing.*

We follow him. He crosses the street, walking ahead of us, turning back in the direction from which we came and passing several stores. Then he sits on a stool in front of one small store. He motions with a tilt of his head for us to enter the store and makes a call on his cell phone. As we enter a tiny crowded shop, a woman says, "Please close the door."

We comply. She waits for a signal on her phone, and opens a concealed rear door. These steps go upstairs. She precedes us, asking us again to please close the door. At the head of the narrow, wooden staircase is a small space, barely large enough for the three of us to stand. Feeling claustrophobic, I see a door that I open, but it is a toilet. I take a few steps back, surprised. Meanwhile the woman walks into a closet, lined with boxes, with shelves on all three walls. She starts rearranging the boxes. I think she is unpacking handbags for us to see. But no, she moves the closed boxes easily. Perhaps they are empty.

Soon the middle shelf is empty and she removes the shelf, revealing an empty wall. Using a key, she opens a door in the wall. She motions us inside with a wave of her hand that holds her phone and departs. There is another young woman inside this very small windowless closet of a room. Designer handbags hang on hooks on three sides of the space. There are boxes below the displays. She asks us what we want. My friend says,

"I'm looking for a black bag, not too big, with a shoulder strap." We don't see any. The saleswoman takes down a quilted black classic Chanel, with a small logo, opens the bag and shows us an extra strap, which can be attached to the bag. It is perfect. Just what my elegant friend would be comfortable toting. But I cannot find one I like in that room. Will we get our price? She quotes a higher price.

I answer, "The man promised me this price." She is quiet for a moment.

"You buy two?" She tries to slip the bag onto my shoulder.

"No, I don't see one I want. Only this one," I answer.

She thinks only for a moment before selling the bag at our price. She packs it in a black plastic bag and opens the door. We wait as she replaces the shelf and the boxes before she opens the door for us to descend. When I look at her questioningly, she shrugs her shoulders and says only, "Police."

Soon we are back on the street with our purchase. Now my friend is feeling as I felt before. "It's not fair that I found a bag and you have not seen one as nice as the first one. Do you want to go back?" she asks.

"Not now, maybe later." We walk on.

I feel as if we are in a spy movie. They are all being so careful and so secretive, communicating with cell phones. *I really don't need a new handbag*, I think.

"It's time for lunch," Marilynn says. She awakens early every day as she has breakfast before her husband

177

leaves for dialysis. As for me, it is still morning. Perhaps I'll have a coffee. We find a corner café several blocks away, with cane-backed chairs and tables open to the sidewalk. The posted menu is written in Italian and features dinner items. The maître d' asks us what we would like and suggests a vegetable panini for my friend for lunch and an omelet for me for breakfast. We are seated, served cappuccinos as we wait for our food and survey the multi- ethnic parade in front of us. We are in Little Italy now. We have had an adventure, a temporary escape from care-giving, on Canal Street in New York City, three blocks from the C train.

26 – The Pile-Up

New York, October 2010

"I'm having a pity party and you're all invited," I announce to the knot of women waiting for the dance instructor at the health club this morning. "It is my twentieth wedding anniversary; I'm having skin cancer surgery Monday, getting hearing aids Wednesday and cataract surgery on the 25th."

"Can I come too?" asks one of the women, someone I barely know.

"Sure," I answer, "The price of admission's a hug."

"The cataract surgery's going to be mighty expensive," says Alison.

"How come? I think the hearing aids cost more," I respond.

"Well no, once my mom could see clearly, she repainted and redecorated the apartment; that cost my dad a fortune." she replies.

"What you have here is a pile-up," adds Charlotte, "and when you have a pile-up, you've got to untangle yourself one layer at a time, slowly, and it'll all sort itself out."

"And the anniversary? Isn't that a good thing?" asks the woman in the green shirt whose name I don't know.

"Well, yesterday, my husband Bob came into the bank while I happened to be there making a deposit," I explain. As I start to talk, I tear up.

"It's a good thing I met you here," he started. "I'm coming to ask the bank to give me all my money they have in here," Bob said, flailing his arms up and down. "Do you hear me? They have to give me all the money."

"Where's Lyle?" I wanted to know where Bob's companion was. "I don't know. He wanted to go for coffee. I don't want coffee. I want my money," Bob's voice is getting louder. I am embarrassed. I look around me, not wanting a scene in the bank, but I don't have a clue as to how to redirect or calm him. While I am thinking about what to do, Bob continues, "No, I want all my money. You can't have ANY of my money anymore; I'm going to talk to someone here at the bank."

I gather up my things from the counter, and try to look calm. Pocketing the deposit envelope I scurry out of the bank, alone, hoping Bob will follow me, but he doesn't. When I get home, I am in a panic. I call Bob's physician.

"You do know, Bob's got a condition," he says patiently. "These things will happen once in a while."

The women in my dance group listen, the one who asked the question starts to tear up as well, and soon I am crying. They all hug me, someone hands me a tissue. "We'll dance it all out. Can't think of anything else while we're learning a new dance."

Putting it all together, I've got one hell of a pile-up today, and a great bunch of health club friends.

27 – Family Thanksgiving

Arizona, November 2010

Folks begin to gather at my daughter Linda's beautiful Arizona house at 2:25 p.m. although the suggested time was three. We're not at grandma's house today, as this family is blessed with three grandmas as well as three grandpas. The desert sand-colored, stucco house, built overlooking the lush green golf course is newly painted. The living room is decorated with a lighted synthetic Christmas tree in the corner. Two leather loveseats flank an entertainment center. A small piano sits on the facing wall. We walk through to the family room and into the hub of the house, the kitchen. I arrive first with my husband. Because he has Alzheimer's disease, it's better for him to be greeted by a few people at a time, and to settle in. Grant, age 7, greets us with big hugs at the door as Dave, his father, peels potatoes at the sink. Dave stops to say hello and give hugs. Linda, my daughter and our hostess, putting more containers into the oven, smiles and says hi. As Bob and I go to retrieve asparagus spears, Bob's famous Thanksgiving Jell-O mold and a vegetable tray from the car, we are greeted by my younger son, Ted, who has just arrived. He helps us unload the car. Grant is also outside, greeting his paternal grandparents, Grammy and Grampy. They treat both boys as their grandsons, enjoying fishing trips and playing board games with them. Today, Grammy Bobbi walks in slowly using a cane. She has severe back pain; her husband Bob has learned over the years that she is often in pain and is now very solicitous of her and caring. He is carrying two large pies, of necessity this year, purchased, not home baked. Bobbi is a terrific cook and her cakes and pies are loved by all.

Bob seats himself on the one end of the wraparound forest green couches, next to Robin, my daughter's first husband who is Austin's father. He injured his knee, so he also has a cane by his side. His leg is raised onto the large rectangular, leather covered ottoman/cocktail table. The men are watching football.

Ted relieves Dave of potato peeling and slicing chores, as mashed potato cooking is his contribution to the meal. Robin brought the roasted turkey. *I wonder how he carried it.* Steve, my older son, walks in with a large green bean casserole. He is barely mobile himself, having recently had back surgery. Dave's brother Mike arrives with his wife, Chris and a baked ham. Robin's parents, called Nana and Pop-Pop, bounce in with rutabagas, yams, chips and dip. Nana Dottie gets busy making gravy while Pop-Pop Idie sits with his son and both Bobs. We are almost all assembled. Austin, our college boy grandson has yet to descend from his bedroom. Gloria, Robin's long-time girlfriend will arrive with her mentally challenged daughter. It is better for Monica to arrive late, and not greet anyone. She prefers to sit quietly observing from behind dark glasses.

Soon the women are gathered around the kitchen island, the cooks on one side, and the observers on the other. Today I am an observer. Everything with my husband has been going smoothly this week. He is not angry; he is more independent, making his omelets or a cup of tea, but we have been together every day for a week, and now that I am here, I feel I don't have to worry about him. There are many people here who know him, know that he has lost his memory to Alzheimer's disease. I feel I can be on a mini-vacation for a few hours. Maybe I'll even have a glass of wine with my dinner. I haven't had a glass of wine in quite a while because Bob seems to have forgotten about alcohol consumption, and that's good.

There is no one older than 7 who is truly comfortable in this mixed family. Each has made an effort to be here and to enjoy the day. Dave offers everyone drinks and the tantalizing appetizers are attacked with fervor. The Hebrew National salami is a big hit. Linda wrapped it in tin foil, roasted it in the oven, after she sliced it in small triangular pieces and coated it with honey mustard sauce, and now she serves it with toothpicks. The carrots and celery with Ranch dressing go well, but the broccoli florets linger on the tray with a few cherry tomatoes. Everyone picks at the chips and dip, as we watch Dave carve the turkey and slice the ham, and we watch Linda spoon the honeyed carrots, yams and roasted asparagus spears with parmesan cheese onto their serving dishes. The rutabagas are already mashed, mildly spiced with nutmeg and need only a spoon. The green bean casserole has been reheated in the microwave oven.

My Bob feels hungry and eats a whole meal of appetizers from the serving dishes, annoying Dottie, who tells Linda, who asks me to "do something" about it. I demur. When we are seated at the tables, Bob eats nothing, just sips on a glass of Riesling wine. I think he has filled up on appetizers. Steve tells me later that Bob did put a small amount of food on his appetizer plate, but then, by accident, sprinkled fish food on his plate, thinking it was salt. He threw the plate in the garbage and ate nothing else.

Austin and Grant are the only children of all these adults. The conversations today center around the boys: Austin's first year at NAU, Northern Arizona University, the snow and ice, whether he is making new friends and how he is experiencing being away from home for the first time. Austin is shy, smiling, but not effusive surrounded by so many avid listeners. We all worried about the effect on him of his parents' divorce when he was seven, Linda's remarriage when he was nine and the birth of Grant when he was almost eleven. Everyone is aware how he has matured this past year and we are all proud of our participation in his growth and development. Now our second grader tells about his Karate lessons after school as well as Suzuki violin lessons and keyboarding class. Grant is also a Cub Scout this year and since he is not shy at all, he shares his stories happily.

The football game is important today, not for any other reason than as a subject for conversation. We discuss Robin's knee injury; that happened yesterday. But when he begins to talk about his hiking, a note of criticism is already heard from his mother, so the conversation stops. Bobbi and Steve discuss medications and surgeries, but when all other conversation stops to listen, they quiet. Dave's father Bob talks to my Bob in a loud voice, as if he were hard of hearing. His wife gets up and whispers to him. He gets quiet. Linda is worrying how everything will get served hot at the same time. Grant only wants to know where Austin will sit, so he can sit next to his brother.

Finally, at 4 p.m., Linda announces dinner. Everyone chooses a place to sit at any of three tables set for six each. Two tables are next to each other between the kitchen and the great room. The second table has been moved in from the patio, as it is too windy to eat outdoors today. The third is in the dining room. Where do I want to sit? I choose the dining room, as it is quieter for my husband. I am also concerned he will say something that might upset Monica. The other four family members already seated in the dining room are Dave's parents, their older son Mike and Chris, his wife. There is no formality this year, no hand holding, no recitations of thankfulness; everyone fills his or her plate and digs in. I for one am very thankful for a lovely family day in which Bob participated as much as he could without any agitation.

28 – Worries

Arizona, December 2010

"The quick brown fox jumps over the lazy dog." I have a new state of the art laptop computer, replacing the one Bob smashed with a book last May. That day still is very present in my mind. I live fearing the medication will cease to work and the angry, irritated Bob will return full force, especially since I found a half pill of his under the table, and Steve thinks Bob threw one set of pills in the garbage this week. I get a glimpse of that behavior sometimes, just to keep my guard up, I guess.

It just worked out that we eat dinner with the children three days in a row. On Sunday we take Austin for Mexican food before he returns to college for exams. He is here for the weekend to attend a high school dance with his girlfriend, Jen. The next night, Dave is out of town, so Linda and Grant are alone. I invite them to join us at home for supper. The following day, Linda rushes her friend to the hospital because her friend's colon was perforated by a polyp removal during a colonoscopy. I pick Grant up at the bus. So Grant eats dinner with us and Steve arrives to take him home to complete his homework before his mother returns.

After dinner, Bob asks, "What is my brother's telephone number?" I tell him. He writes the numbers down.

"That's nice, Bob, to call Irving." We've been in Arizona for three weeks and he hasn't wanted to talk to his brother or to invite Irving to visit us this winter.

"I just want to talk to him, that's all," was Bob's answer. He goes into the bathroom for privacy, but he doesn't close the door all the way, so I hear him complaining to his brother.

"I'm ready to go back to New York. Her children are here all the time, all of them, sometimes one, sometimes another." After his phone call, Bob went to bed early. He was clearly upset. But in the morning, I heard no more about it.

Yesterday I felt another fearful moment, after Bob had an insightful one. I ask Bob to come with me to a hair appointment. He says, "I'd prefer to remain home alone." I explain that I will be going to the gym from 8 until 9, and then I will be home for an hour, before driving to the hairdresser from 10 to 10:30 for my 10:30 to 12:30 appointment.

"That's too long for me to be here by myself. Don't go to the gym. From 10 to 1 will be long enough for me to be here by myself." I am amazed by his awareness, his recognition of his limits and I take a short walk in the neighborhood instead. When I return he is showered and dressed.

"I changed my mind. I will go with you," he says in a teasing, playful voice. "Wherever you go, I go."

"I'm happy to have you. We'll stop and buy doughnuts and coffee on the way. Please bring your newspaper, so you have something you are interested in to read while you wait for me."

Bob is fine for the first hour. The salon is busy; there are many people to watch, not all women. They all love sharing our "munchkin" donut donation. The doughnuts are on a coffee table in front of the chair Bob sits in, so each person talks with him when they take a donut. Then he begins to get restless, making non-verbal gestures with his hands. Dressed in my color processing splendor, I ask what he wants.

"What do you mean, what do I want? I want to get out of here! When are we leaving?" The angry tone is back again. I worry he will make a scene, but pointing to my head I say, "Gee, Hon, I'm sorry, but we have to wait for my hair to be finished before we can leave."

Bob begins to pace around the shop. Manda, my stylist and the owner of the salon, walks up to him.

"Bob, would you like to sit outside? There's a patio in the sunshine close by. Shall I show it to you?"

Crisis averted. Bob follows Manda and remains outside for quite a while. When he walks back in, he has another cup of coffee and says to Manda when she asks,

"I'd go home if I could; I need to get outside to take care of my plants."

Each of these little scary episodes shakes me, causes my heart to skip a beat, reminds me how fragile his hold on his emotions is and how fragile I am becoming. When my children were teenagers, they gave me a hard time, too. As a single parent, I had to be both nurturer and disciplinarian to kids who were by that time taller and heavier than me. They were sometimes angry with me, but I was tough. I overheard Linda once on the telephone telling a friend, "I'd love to go. But you know how my mother is. She'd never let me." Linda had never even asked me that time. I cannot be tough anymore. I am always worried.

Luckily for me, I don't do advance worrying. Some folks fret about things that might happen in the future. I have enough to worry about in the present. This is dental checkup week. Bob has an abscess in one tooth which needs to be capped; the neighboring tooth is chipped, it needs to be refilled. Bob is no longer brushing his teeth consistently. I can't always remind him to brush as one would a child; he is an adult and besides, he doesn't remember that he didn't brush his teeth. Sometimes I see that he has merely rinsed his mouth with mouthwash instead of brushing and the floss is not used anymore unless a piece of food gets stuck. Then he will dig at it, in public without concern for others who may be forced by proximity to watch. I now hand him floss, even in a restaurant. I try showing Bob the dry toothbrush as evidence that it hadn't been wet, but he just shrugs his shoulders. So he suffers the pain of dental work and we pay the fees.

The next worry is his physical health. For two days the week we left New York, Bob slept, ingesting barely anything. He pointed to his throat, that it hurt, then to his chest. I felt his head; he seemed to have a fever so I gave him Tylenol and weak tea. By Wednesday, I knew he had to see the physician. Our physician in New York is located on the same block as our apartment building, so I phoned, made an appointment for later on Wednesday and Dr. A. checked Bob out. Everything was fine, including an EKG, so he took a blood sample to check further. Bob's condition improved and we came to Arizona. Bob's laboratory report followed us. Bob's iron is low, his calcium and blood counts are all low. This is a significant change since September. We returned to see Dr. R., our Arizona internist, this week. He ordered new blood work and we are waiting to see what might need to be done next.

29 – *Memory Loss Awareness*

Arizona, December 2010

"I don't know anything anymore," says Bob while we drive in the car to the farmer's market. "I don't know why the clouds form the way they do, or the names of the different ones. I used to." He pauses and continues, "I've forgotten everything I used to know. Where did it all go?"

Each time we drive in the car, we admire the configuration of the clouds in this huge Arizona sky. The clouds are so beautiful, sometimes puffy and white, other times wispy or streaks of white against a deep, almost Italian blue sky. I am continually soothed by their beauty. I feel privileged to be able to admire this wonderful countryside, so different from the East coast where I spent most of my life. Bob, unfortunately sees the same panorama, but attends to his losses.

"I know, dear," I answer soothingly, I hope, "I am so sorry this is happening to you. I wish we could fix it."

"I used to read a lot, but I don't even do that anymore. I picked up two books in the library yesterday, and today I seem to have lost interest in them. I don't know why I bought them."

So it seems we lose another weekly activity that used to be pleasing; we would drive to the library, me to return and borrow books on my list and Bob to peruse the sale books, to find some non-fiction subject that strikes his fancy. Maybe next week he will enjoy the library again. Luckily he is maintaining an interest in his workshop, sorting, storing, finding and misplacing his tools. He is also avidly watering and fertilizing the bushes and trees, hoping to undo the "damage" the gardeners inflicted during our absence by cutting back the growth too severely. I also try to keep up his interest in food and food preparation.

"We'll have a good time at the market. You are great at picking out good fruits and vegetables." I try to change the subject also because ruminating on lost skills is unhelpful. *It is so sad to lose one's memory, but to be aware of the loss is so much more painful.* I can't change the topic to a memory of times spent together. I can't provide the knowledge he is looking for. I can't tell him of a future event that he could look forward to. All of those abilities are also gone. He only remembers an event if something within him triggers the memory; if I give him the answer about cumulous cloud formations, he won't go "right, thanks", he wouldn't understand what I am saying, perhaps even forgetting what he has just said. And if I tell him Steve is coming for dinner and bringing barbecued chicken, and we're getting the side dishes to go along with it, he might answer, "Who is Steve?"

At the Superstition Ranch market, named for the Superstition Mountains that loom above us a few miles east, we both act as if we're in a candy store and our parent has said we could buy whatever we wish. The produce comes from Mexico and the prices are so reasonable, we always buy more than we can possibly eat, but no problem, we can share with the family.

Iceberg lettuce at three heads for a dollar, those long plastic-wrapped burp-less cucumbers which cost $ 1.99 each in New York in the summer are also three for a dollar; and celery, which costs almost three dollars for one bunch in New York, here are also three for a dollar. We buy grapes at 99 cents a pound, as well as apples, Bosc pears and Anjou pears, bananas and loads of green beans, plus a pound of fresh spinach for 59 cents. In December, no less. We come home and prepare an all veggie dinner, two ears of white corn each (six for a dollar) mashed potatoes, spinach sautéed with olive oil and garlic, fresh green salad and lots of scraps to save for Tortellini, Steve's turtle.

Steve is stuck in traffic and will bring the chicken tomorrow, as Bob now needs to eat dinner by 5:30.

In New York, Bob would take an afternoon nap, or more frequently, stay in pajamas and snooze all morning. Here he is awake by seven a.m., and usually asleep before 9 p.m., often in his chair keeping me company while I read or watch television or a movie. Last night, we watched a Charlie Chaplin movie, "The Gold Rush", which kept Bob's interest for quite a while, but not until the end. As he got up from his chair he said, "I don't know what's going on," and he went to bed. I think Bob understood the plot and knew that the little guy got rich by helping the prospector. But when Charlie Chaplin donned his old clothes once more on the ship, Bob got confused and quit.

Generally, Arizona is better for Bob now, as the warm weather combined with the fresh air and the ease of access to the outside from our single level home, keeps him awake during the day and permits him to sleep, without snoring for a full ten to twelve hours each night. His needs for adventure are met by trips to the stores with me and his need for other people to talk with seems to be met by my children stopping by, or meeting them in a restaurant for dinner. Bob has developed a taste for diner food these past four years. Since the diagnosis, Bob reports that his taste buds "have stopped working" and he prefers highly spiced food. He says he doesn't appreciate the subtleties of nuanced taste any longer. We used to splurge on fancy restaurant dinners once in a while, and on esoteric ingredients that Bob cooked at home, but now all he wants is Village Inn's *huevos rancheros*, or Applebee's *Asian chicken*. He also likes chicken quesadillas or tacos at a Mexican restaurant. We found one Chinese restaurant, the Lychee Inn, which he enjoys and where he eats heartily. Since all of his choices are for reasonably priced, family-style restaurants, it is well within our budget to frequent them and fill a few hours by preparing to leave, driving, filling the gas tank with fuel along the way, eating, stopping perhaps for milk and doughnuts after the meal and then driving home.

While Bob concentrates on his losses, I am amazed by what he remembers. Each time we drive, Bob asks about the gasoline level and about tire pressure. Every morning, Bob remembers the seven o'clock rule, and if he wakes before that, gets his robe and slippers and retrieves the newspaper from the driveway. If he wakes at seven or after, he rolls over for a hug and a back scratch before getting out of bed. He needs no assistance with self-care skills, although he permits me to manage the medications for him now and to serve him his meals. When I do not snap into action when he is hungry, he makes himself a cup of tea, using the electric teapot. He still will make himself a cheese omelet or a salami sandwich, but he doesn't add a small salad or a pickle or other sides, except toast. For dinner, Bob will make salad when asked; he peels potatoes, slices garlic. When we sit to eat, however, Bob no longer eats his salad first, then his main course followed by dessert. His fork choices are random; he wants all of the food on the table at the same time, not liking to see me jump up from the table and he chooses his food with his own fork from the serving bowls.

30 – Leon's Story

Arizona, December 2010

I walk into an Alzheimer's Support group meeting late; the ongoing conversation concerns participants' feelings about caregivers having relationships outside of their marriage to a demented spouse. The leader tries to elicit feelings of guilt or anger, but is getting nowhere.

"Is anyone concerned about what others may think if your spouse is still alive? Would you worry about being seen with someone other than your spouse?" the leader wants to know.

There are 18 to 20 caregivers in the room, most spousal. Many are men. Some have spouses already in a residential care facility where the healthy spouse goes daily to feed and be with the ill one. The leader polls the room. All agree the most isolating part of spousal caregiving for Alzheimer's disease people is not having the spouse as confidant any longer. All report their wish to have someone, anyone to talk with, to take their mind off the daily difficulty and loneliness of being a spousal caregiver. Leon walks in the door. There are no more spaces around the table. The leader grabs a chair and places it at the end of one of the tables which are in a u-shape.

"Welcome. Come sit here, or in the back if you wish to hide." says the leader.

Leon looks at me and says, "Are you staying?"

The leader asks, "Are you together?"

Leon responds, "Yes, but I can't stay. Can you?" he looks at me again.

"Actually, I can't stay. I have to pick my grandson up at the bus stop at 2:30." I answer.

I turn toward the leader. "I thought the caregivers group began at 1 p.m. so we have been here for over an hour already."

"That is a general caregiver's group, sponsored by the Multigenerational Center. The two o'clock group is sponsored by the Alzheimer's Association," the leader explains. I hate to be the center of this mini-drama, disrupting the group. I grab the paperwork off the table, find my purse and follow Leon out the door. The leader calls out after us, "Please bring the paperwork with you next time when you come."

So who is Leon, you are wondering about now, right? I went shopping at our local supermarket the other day by myself, just to pick up a few things I needed to make the Thanksgiving Jell-O mold. I hear a man speaking very solicitously to a woman halfway down the aisle from him.

"Come along, Shirley," he cajoles. I look up and see that he is tall man with a ruddy complexion, a shock of white hair and sturdily built; Shirley, too, is tall, blond, slightly stooped, smiling and walking slowly toward her husband. *This man is a potential person to interview for my care-giving memoir*. He winks at me. I walk up to him and introduce myself.

"I think we are in the same boat," I say. "I am writing a book about my experiences caring for my husband who has Alzheimer's disease. Would you be willing to be interviewed for my book?"

"It is so good to see someone who understands what I'm going through," he says. "Sure, my name is Leon, and this here is Shirley. Actually," he continues, "when I saw you looking at me, I thought you were thinking how condescending I was, talking to my wife like that. I was quite relieved when you came to speak with me." I give him my card and ask him to call me. He says he will call after the holiday.

The following day is Thanksgiving, and on Friday morning, the phone rings. It's Leon.

I haven't thought this through. How will I pursue this interview? Our spouses can't be present. Yet, I can't meet with a stranger alone.

So I invite Leon and Shirley to visit, after lunch on Monday. We'll have to get to know each other. The information I need will develop slowly, over time, if we all feel comfortable.

Shirley and Bob are the same age, 81; their birthdays are only a few weeks apart. Shirley is the eldest of three sisters; she has been diagnosed with Alzheimer's disease for six years. Leon helps her out of the car, closing the door behind her. When they enter, he helps her take off her sweater and directs her where to sit on the couch. She smiles at me, but I doubt she remembers me from the supermarket. I introduce myself and call Bob in from his office. Bob looks understandably confused. He doesn't know these people, has no clue why they are here.

"Bob, this is Leon and his wife Shirley. They live in Canada and are in Arizona for the winter just like we are. Leon was a police officer and he and Shirley met because Shirley also worked at the police department. They are looking to make new friends as we are too. So I invited them to come and visit. Come sit."

Bob's sitting, but he's not saying anything. He looks bewildered. Leon describes the mobile home park they live in and shares the story of their Thanksgiving group meal in the clubhouse; the management provides the turkeys and the residents add side dishes and desserts. There are several other Canadian couples whom they have known for years. He describes a cozy, friendly environment where they have spent winters for the past ten years. They drive down from British Columbia in four days. Leon says he has tapes of songs Shirley likes to sing, and she keeps him entertained as he drives. As if on cue, Shirley begins to sing. We all smile a minute and listen. She sings a few bars and then forgets.

"Bathroom breaks are tough," he continues, "There are sometimes no ladies around me that I can ask to take care of her in the bathroom. On the road there are very few family rest room facilities."

I offer and serve tea, chocolate cake and sliced oranges. The first fruit I buy when we arrive in Arizona are oranges; the ones on our tree are not yet ripe. Leon sits next to Shirley, cuts her orange slice and her cake, and removes her teabag from the cup. She smiles sweetly but does almost nothing for herself. *I hope this man is Catholic; he is eligible in my book for sainthood already.*

Leon tells us he plays golf on the two golf courses on the Viewpoint property. He also plays tennis, but right now he is only practicing with the automatic ball machine.

"Who stays with Shirley when you golf?" I ask.

"She sits in the cart and comes with me," Leon answers smiling.

"And tennis?" I ask.

"Shirley sits and watches me hit the balls."

Bob is sitting at the table, sipping tea and listening, but he still hasn't said anything to our guests. He didn't respond to their mention of Vancouver, where we visited in 1989.

All of a sudden, he pops up like a jack-in-the-box at the end of the jingle, saying to Leon, "Enough of this girl talk. Let's you and me go into the garage and see my tools."

He leads Leon, who follows smiling out to the garage. Shirley also stands, wanders aimlessly in the living room, mumbling under her breath. She is clearly uncomfortable when she cannot see Leon, so we follow them out to the garage. Bob begins to interact with Shirley, too, showing her his collection of tools, neatly arrayed on their designated shelves. He is animated, but we can see that Shirley is restless and Leon decides it is time for him to take her home. Leon promises to continue our conversation via email so we can figure out a way to talk of his experiences for the book.

Leon calls the next day to thank me for our hospitality.

"I miss not having anyone to talk with about all this," he confides. "In Vancouver there's a support group I go to once in a while, and that helps. I get good tips and ideas, but here, there's nothing."

"Actually, there is a group that meets on Fridays, twice a month where I go to the gym," I offer. "I've not yet been able to get out of the house in the afternoon, but I'll find out and maybe we can arrange something. Do you have anyone who could stay with Shirley so you could attend?"

Leon emails me that he has found someone to sit with Shirley. I hire Larry to spend the afternoon with Bob. I even find a new thrift store for them to visit. At the last minute, Bob refuses to go with Larry, says he'd prefer to stay home alone, so I am with some fear and trepidation in the gym by myself at 1 p.m.

Room 5 is empty and dark. The counselor at the social services desk knows nothing; Leon walks in and I am embarrassed that I had arranged this meeting for no good reason. There is a senior center volunteer-run coffee cart and wrought iron tables, some with partially completed jig-saw puzzles. There is music coming from one all-purpose room. Folks are in there dancing. The other all-purpose room holds many card tables; all are occupied by card-playing seniors.

We sit at a table in the main thoroughfare and before I get a chance to apologize, Leon says, "I'm sorry I am late. I went out for a few minutes this morning, telling Shirley to have a sleep-in; I'll be right back. But when I got back, Shirley wasn't there. I looked all over and then I heard a neighbor and another person I don't even know, call 'Leon'. When I went to see, they said Shirley was walking through the back yards toward the club-house. I found her okay. She had put her jeans on back-wards; she still had on her pajama top and slippers."

He settled back into his chair, took a sip of his cof-fee, exhausted.

"I'm so sorry you had such a hard time trying to get to a meeting that isn't even happening," I begin.

"Well, I appreciate this, even sitting here talking with you."

"Has Shirley wandered often?" I ask. "Luckily, Bob hasn't wandered yet. He's just gotten lost in Wal-Mart, which scared me."

"She's just started this business, like in the super-market. She sort of gets lost inside herself and doesn't know where she was headed. Can I ask you something?" Leon sounds desperate.

"Sure," I answer.

"We had a terrible incident in the bathroom. She had a bowel movement, and the face cloth was soiled and I saw traces of it on the floor. It was a mess."

"Oh boy, I'm so sorry you are dealing with this now. You do know that bathroom issues are the number one reason people enter out-of-home care."

"That's what I'm afraid of. She's such a sweetie. But I can't handle this. So tell me, do girls wipe from front to back or from the back like guys do? Shirley seems to be wiping from the front and getting all messed up. She can get an infection that way, can't she?"

We continue talking about practical care-giving is-sues, Canadian nursing home waiting lists and Shirley's sisters who have been willing to take her for a weekend once in a while to their home a few hours away. I mention that there is an adult day care facility attached to this multi-generational center and I show him where it is, and introduce him to the on-site manager, Rosemary, whom I have already met. Just then, the woman counselor tells us there is an Alzheimer support group that will meet in 10 minutes if we are interested. I introduce Leon to Rosemary and excuse myself to attend the support group.

Am I concerned that the people in the Alzheimer's support group think Leon and I are "together"? Did I just write these pages to them, explaining myself? I see how people cover up in groups until they feel comfortable enough to share their true feelings. I actually winced when Leon said that we were together. Of course he had no idea about the topic under discussion. Did that matter? Would I have felt differently had he known or had the subject been different?

31 – Scary New Behavior

Arizona, December 2010

Have you ever been awakened from a deep sleep by the burglar alarm blasting at you? That's what happened here this morning at 6:32 a.m. I jumped out of bed, ran over to the alarm box and dialed what I thought was the code, in order to stop the shrieking. It wasn't. I haven't used the code for a long time. I had to phone my son with the noise shattering my ear drums. First I had to find my cell phone. The land line was temporarily disabled by the alarm company. Steve woke up enough to tell me the code and the alarm was silenced. Whew! I have been shaking all over all morning. The alarm does wake a person up and warn of danger.

This danger I am afraid will continue. Bob looks puzzled. "I thought I was turning on the lights," he says quietly. No remorse, no excitement, no emotional reaction that I could see. "Just the facts, ma'am, just the facts," as Jack Webb from "Dragnet" would say.

Coincidently I read a blog by another Alzheimer spouse last night. My go-to site for help with my caregiving concerns, thealzheimerspouse.com, was rated 20th in helpfulness out of a list of 50 Alzheimer-related websites. I wanted to see which site was rated above this one, which, in my humble opinion, outranks all the other caregiver sites for spouses, primarily because the message boards are so inclusive and easy to access when I need an answer to a specific problem.

Anyway, I opened a blog by a wife who recently placed her husband in a small foster care home. The blog is called "A Day in Dementiaville." She noted her husband's aberrant behaviors, such as urinating in inappropriate places, leaving home unattended, moving all the furniture around, biting her hand when she went to feed him; my dreams last night were filled with the possibilities that are ahead of me. I am trying to enjoy the respite we are experiencing now, but it is hard. I am always wondering what will come next. Steve saw a huge penknife in Bob's pocket yesterday. When Bob saw Steve looking at it, Bob hid the knife. Luckily I found it after Bob went to sleep and I re-hid it for now. He has been sharpening knives in Arizona, as he had in New York. He hasn't done anything with them, but I fear for our safety.

My friends and cousins are concerned for me; except for three trips to the gym each week, I have not resumed any independent activity away from home. The first time Larry, the caregiver, arrived since we returned to Arizona, he was supposed to come just for a visit. But Bob wanted to go with him, so they went shopping. The next time, Bob refused when Larry called to set up a date. I am afraid to set up another date with Larry. I don't want Bob to get upset. Intellectually, I know it is the increased medication that is keeping Bob calm; emotionally I fear I could ruin this peacefulness by asserting my need for independence. I am not even reading or working on my writing, as Bob asks me repeatedly to help redirect him ("I don't know what to do") or to help him find something he has misplaced. Actually, the items are often in their proper place. Bob merely forgets where they are. Always, he asks where I put something or other, or claims someone has been in his workshop and moved items, until I find them.

The other day we went holiday shopping together and Bob bought himself a pullover sweater. He never wears the ones that are stashed in drawers in New York, yet he wears this grey sweater non-stop for a few days, clearly loving this sweater. Yesterday he came to me looking for it. We search the entire house unsuccessfully, until bedtime when I find the sweater under his pillow with his pajamas. Sometimes he doesn't put things back in their proper place and it becomes my game to play "hide and seek." I ran to the store after the gym this morning to buy index cards. I wrote on one ALARM and on the other KITCHEN LIGHTS. I hope it helps prevent this morning's problem from recurring.

I guess I started to get fearful when I met with Leon at the Multigenerational Center last week. Leon is the man I met at the supermarket before Thanksgiving, whose wife has Alzheimer's disease. His wife's dressing and wandering behavior have just begun to deteriorate six years after her diagnosis. I had believed, when told that 60% of Alzheimer's disease patients wander, that, since Bob has not wandered, he wouldn't. Now of course I am not so sure. Here in Mesa, Arizona, Bob is safe around our home; there are no predators. In New York I am worried someone might harm him, or rob him. In our gated community, if he wanders, he may not be able to find his way home. I walk with him from home to the mailbox and back, both ways, on the perimeter sidewalk and through the streets of the subdivision. I point out the flags at the community entrance each time we enter or depart and I have Bob open the mailbox at the gate and check for mail each day. I guess a wandering problem has to occur before I hire someone to stay here with him all day every day so I can leave with a free mind.

32 – Alex's Story

Arizona, December 2010

Today is Alzheimer's Support Group day. The group meets on alternate Friday afternoons at the Multi-Generational Center in Mesa. Bob is fertilizing the plants in our backyard, alone. I arrive at 1:40, not wanting to be late for my second meeting. James is a member of the group who is already seated and anxious to begin talking. I know his name as he has placed a name card in front of him on the table. It seems as if the folks who attend this meeting regularly return each time with their name cards.

"This is the only time I have to be away from my wife of 61 years, who doesn't recognize me some days and always wants to go "home" to New Hampshire, where she has not lived since we got married. She wants to see her 11 siblings, ten of whom are long gone."

"Who's with her now?" I ask.

"I hire a housekeeper. She comes twice a month to clean. She gets there at 12:30 and I have to be back by 3:30. She gets $ 20 an hour, but I pay her $ 80 each week and this week it'll be $160 for her Christmas. She's been with me for a year and a half and my wife's used to her, so that's why I keep her."

"I'm trying to find someone who will do that for me now, but the women I have spoken with all want to be home by 2:30 p.m. to get their children from the school bus," I add.

"I'm going to keep my wife with me until she passes. I'm never going to put her in any of those homes I've seen."

Leon walks in, sits next to me. James begins to speak of a fall he's had this week, shows us his arm which is bruised and bandaged, his wrist is blue. He is 91 years young and he fell on the cement on Sunday. His wife, a former nurse, questions him each day about what he is doing, wrapping his arm, but shows no memory for his fall, or sadness that he is hurt. I do, but obviously not enough, for, as the group assembles and Mary takes the lead in the absence of the social worker, James pops up in response to a question to tell something good that has transpired this week, showing everyone his bandaged arm. Nothing good has happened in his life, this week or for a long time. But this accident certainly made the week different. Once again I see how important it is for us caregivers to speak with others who have similar lonely lives, caring for a spouse who can no longer provide emotional support or even listen to our concerns.

Bill arrives, then Sara, Ann, Paula and Hope. Each puts a name card on the table. Leon asks, "Have any of your spouses had problems with mirrors?"

"Shirley my wife," says Leon, "has been diagnosed with Alzheimer's disease now for six years. She is upset that other women are in her home," he continues, "not believing that the person she sees in the mirror is herself. She doesn't want to undress in the bathroom, as others are in there." Unfortunately, the wall in their bedroom is mirrored, hiding the closet doors. Shirley has wandered to the neighbor's house, complaining that there are women in hers. The neighbor brings Shirley home, but seems to wonder if Leon does indeed have other women home. People just don't understand.

Mary's husband has been attending the Arbor Rose Day Care Center for two years. The Veteran's Administration pays for 20 hours of his day care every week. Today Mary is happy; she reports that her husband just received permanent disability status from the Veteran's Administration. There will be money to fix up their house and to pay bills. But, she worries; will the VA be in charge of her husband's money? Will she have to petition the VA to purchase a new refrigerator? No one knows the answer. Her husband no longer recognizes himself in the mirror, but has not given a name to what he thinks the reflection is.

Ann has an aunt who raised her; she is now 99 years old and living in a group home. She is the only one here today who is not a spousal caregiver. Alex and an older woman walk in late and say nothing during the entire first hour. The others seem to know them, yet no one has asked them a question. The discussion shifts to bathroom issues, a topic which elicits many suggestions. Everyone has some issues and some remedies here. A substitute social worker enters, but she allows the conversation already begun, to continue. As people begin to leave, I ask Alex who he cares for. We sit entranced for another half hour, listening to his story.

"My name is Alex and this is my mother Louise," he begins. "We've known something is the matter with my dad for the past six or seven years, but the problem is my mother." Louise is pale, wan, tired looking. Her face

Is set in a mask, expressionless. She wears a hospital identification tag on her right wrist. She says nothing. She looks straight ahead, not at her son who is seated to her right.

Alex, wearing a blue dress shirt with long sleeves, is well groomed, young and has a wireless Bluetooth telephone receiver in his ear. He sometimes pats his mother on the back as he speaks, but does not look at her. Basically, his eyes are on me, as I asked the leading question.

"With the 20-20 of hindsight, I can now see that something was wrong with my dad back in '97, before I moved out here in 2000. Anyway, my parents moved out here from Seattle to be near my sister. They live in Tennessee now. My dad was an aeronautic engineer. He could point out the pros and cons of any position and form conclusions. But six years ago, he and my mom got in the car and drove back to Seattle. I got a call from Seattle, my dad saying he can't live in Arizona anymore. 'Arizona's a hell hole', he yelled into the phone when he called me from there. Since my dad had given up driving before that, my mom drove the entire way. By the time they arrived, she had to be hospitalized; her back had given out."

Alex doesn't stop to take a breath. He informs us of his parents' frequent moves from Seattle to Phoenix and back again, putting their furniture in storage, retrieving it, buying a condo, renovating the condo. He is getting more agitated as he speaks and more forceful. His mother sits still, says nothing. Her facial expression doesn't change. She has heard this all before.

"But the problem is my mom. I have begged, cajoled, asked her to take him to the doctor; at the last minute she cancels the appointments saying my dad doesn't want to go. She won't do anything I ask of her; she listens to my dad to her own detriment."

"Who is with your dad now?" I ask. *It seems the others have heard this story before. Why is Alex getting so red in the face if this is an old story that has already been solved?*

"He's in day care."

"Then your mom did listen eventually," I add.

"Yes, last August she finally agreed after driving again up to Seattle and having him call as soon as they got there that he wanted to come back again to Phoenix. And five days after my father was finally diagnosed with Alzheimer's disease, she was diagnosed with multiple myeloma, a blood cancer." Alex is almost in tears. "All because of the physical and mental stress she had been under for all these years." I understand now why they arrived late and why he is so upset. They have just returned from a hospital treatment.

I can certainly relate to Alex. His father's behavior sounds like Bob's. When we're in New York, he wants to be in Arizona. Now that we're here, he says he's ready to go back to New York. I have to show him the news broadcast that proves how much ice and wind and cold there is in New York now, just as I had to show him it was too hot in Arizona for us to return here sooner last summer.

I also know how persuasive Bob can be when he is making a point, and how used he is to getting his way in an argument. *Will I too look like Louise in a few years? But I catch myself.* Now Louise speaks in a small, thin voice.

"Can I say a few words in my own defense?" she asks.

"Sure," the chorus of voices around the table urges her to speak.

"Well," she begins, "I was born and brought up in northern Idaho. We girls didn't get much education then, and I never felt I was as smart or as well educated as my husband, so I felt I had to let him make all the big decisions in our family. And after living that way for so many years, it is not possible to change very easily."

Louise speaks well, she is thoughtful as she continues, "Last summer, we were up in Seattle again, my husband called Alex and he got off the phone, crying. 'Louise', he said, 'there really is something the matter with me. I am not thinking clearly. When we get back to Phoenix, I will go see your doctor.' I was tired of going back and forth from Seattle to Phoenix all the time, so I was glad he finally made the decision."

"Louise, that must have been the hardest thing for you to realize," I said.

Then Leon added, "The hardest thing with me about my wife was losing her as a confidante, not having her to talk things over with anymore."

"If Alex wasn't around to take care of things now, I don't know what I'd do." she concludes.

People have been quietly leaving during this conversation. I too, have to leave. Bob has been home by himself for two hours. Paula's cell phone beeps. Paula has not contributed to today's conversation at all. Since she has a name card, I assume she is a regular attendee at these meetings.

"It's my master's voice," she says, "calling to say I've been out long enough, come home already." She wishes everyone a happy holiday and leaves saying,

"I'll see you all next year."

33 – Overly Significant Everyday Experiences

Arizona, January 2011

I thought it would be nice to have a picture of us as a couple. It has been several years since we posed for a photo for folks to remember us by, and we certainly look different now. Our synagogue initiated a fund raiser this year. In cooperation with a professional photographer, the synagogue would publish a photo directory to facilitate the 550 member families getting to know each other better. Bob was not happy to dress in a white long sleeved shirt; it is Arizona after all. But he was mollified when I said he could wear his jeans and sneakers. Jeans, sneakers and a colorful short-sleeved shirt is his local uniform lately. He always looks groomed, so his choice of colorful shirt is usually fine with me. But the photographer said long sleeves and the same color for both of us, so our choice was narrowed.

In the morning, I tell Bob we will leave here at 12:30 for a 1:30 appointment a half hour away. I have 30 minutes leeway for last minute delays and Bob is agreeable as it leaves him an hour to water and fertilize his plants before he has to come in to shower and dress. At 11:30, when I remind him, he's compliant, if not thrilled. By 12:15 he's ready, but I'm not. I'm still fussing with hair and makeup. I still have fifteen minutes.

At 12:30 I'm ready and Bob says he's hungry. I announce we're going out for lunch after the setting, but that's not sufficient. When Bob's hungry these days, he wants food *now*. So I get out an already hard-cooked egg, a left-over biscuit and I prepare a cup of tea, thinking this will hold him until lunch. At 12:45, I ask him to meet me in the car, please.

After all my worrying, we arrive on time and the photographer is late! Bob is still hungry and not in a mood to sit quietly. The secretary notices his discomfort and offers him water ("no thanks, I don't drink water") and a cookie, which he eats as he sits, posture slouched, facial expression blank. Other people enter, also waiting for a photo shoot. I strike up a conversation with a professor at ASU and a woman who lives at an assisted living facility nearby. She and her family will have their family photo taken with their ancient, blind and deaf wire-haired fox terrier. I have no time schedule; I am not anxious about the photographer's lateness, but the secretary is. She phones but receives no response. Now she begins to be concerned for his safety. She calls an alternate photographer to fill in. After a full half hour someone arrives. No explanation is offered; we don't know if this is the original or the replacement person. No one asks. The professor asks to be first as he is on a schedule. We are called next.

Bob follows me into the adjacent room where there is a screen used as a backdrop, a stool and several boxes painted black. He is utterly confused. He has forgotten why we are here and questions the environment. "What room is this? There's nothing here for me to see. Why

216

are you bringing me here? What are you DOING to me?" This is a frequent refrain when Bob feels insecure.

"Sir, please sit on the stool facing me," requests the photographer.

"Why should I do that? It doesn't even look like a comfortable place to sit."

"And ma'am, if you would, please stand here, placing an arm on your husband's shoulder," he continues, smiling. "This won't take a minute."

"Sir, please turn your head towards me, and loo k over my left shoulder." Bob just sits there. The photographer comes close to Bob and tries to position his head. He turns toward me, "Excuse me, but is your husband deaf?"

"No, he can hear you, but he has Alzheimer's disease and he seems to be confused." The photographer changes gears and begins to snap pictures, which focuses Bob, who finally seems to understand what is happening and smiles cooperatively.

After the couple photograph is taken, separate snaps are shot of each of us, we are shown the digital images on a computer and we are asked to choose which we prefer. Bob is upset.

"Why is there a white spot on my head?" he asks. I mumble something about the lighting and the highlights, but the salesman, who is not the photographer, looks at Bob and says, "Sir, I hate to tell you, but your hair is grey. Just look in the mirror." Surprisingly, Bob is quiet, we order copies for each of the children and we leave to go for lunch.

34 – Out in Limbo-Dismissed by the Movement Disorders Clinic

Arizona, January 2011

"I don't have any daughters," announces Bob to the neurologist, Dr. L., who is asking him questions as she performs a routine Parkinson's Tasks of Daily Living Assessment.

"And do you have any sons?" Dr. L. asks.

"Yes," answers Bob tilting his head as requested.

"What are their names?" asks the doctor.

"Steve," Bob says. Then, reconsidering, "No, that's not right. Adam, yes, Adam is my son." He rests for a moment and continues, "And there are some grandchildren, too."

My son Steve is sitting next to me at the visit to the Movement Disorders Clinic today, listening to Bob's responses. Mainly I want him to see the beautiful facility, but I also need company for the ride, the visit and lunch. Bob cannot carry on a conversation any longer and to spend the day driving for an hour to a doctor visit with him by myself is tedious.

Bob was unable to answer any of the Mini Mental exam questions. He quipped, "I guess the only thing I know anymore is my name." *Imagine being Bob, being aware of not remembering.*

Of course he did try to cover his lack of knowledge by his usual reference to the New York Times, as well as pretending he had watched the State of the Union address the previous evening. Actually, he has spent the hour in his library as Steve and I watched.

The doctors dismissed Bob from the neurology service after the visit, refusing to write a new prescription, referring him, instead, to the psychiatrist on their unit who specializes in dementia. But the psychiatrist was not in and so we have to wait to schedule another appointment and drive to Phoenix again. The physicians, a married pair of older neurologists, were very friendly and compassionate, convincingly talking about day care placement for Bob. Dr. L. looked quite tanned, as if he spends more time on the golf course these days than in his practice. I will miss these visits. Really, I miss the diagnosis, as Parkinson's disease can be better controlled than Alzheimer's disease.

I follow up with the request to the psychiatrist's office for an appointment. I am told there has been no referral from the neurologist; I am to seek services at the Alzheimer Institute instead. I call there, and I'm told they will first send me a packet of information to be filled out and returned before they will set up a visit, but not for the psychiatrist, for a complete evaluation. I don't want to put Bob through another evaluation, but I have nowhere else to turn here in Phoenix. I feel I may need stronger medication if I insist he go to Day Care and Bob is not willing.

Meanwhile, I have complied with all the requirements for the day care club. Bob had a chest x-ray on Tuesday after a three hour visit to the club on Monday, followed by a doctor's visit today so that Dr. R. could fill out the required forms. Tomorrow we will go to the club again, and I will leave Bob there while I attend the caregiver's group at the multi-generational center. This is not yet respite for me.

The Alzheimer Institute sends me a packet of information to fill out and return by fax, after my signature has been witnessed. Then they will schedule an initial assessment. I will speak with a social worker while Bob undergoes cognitive testing. Then we will see the psychiatrist. The appointment is scheduled for March 16, six weeks hence. Bob's agitation is increasing. We have had no change in medication for several months. I am afraid but I seem to have no choice but to wait six more weeks.

35 – Metaphor for My Life Today

Arizona, January 2011

I am on my way home by myself, from Blockbusters, the video store, where I have exchanged "The Lemon Tree" for "After the Wedding". My car trip is easy; enter the Arizona Red Mountain Freeway at McDowell Drive, stay in the right lane for one exit a mile down the road, exit and I'm one mile from home. So, I am not paying complete attention. I'm thinking how grateful I am to Steve for this gift of movies to watch after Bob has retired for the night. As the exit ramp appears and the road widens, I stay in the left lane, as my turn around the traffic circle requires. Ahead of me, I see a red boxy car, coming right at me. That snaps me to attention. My first thought is that I am in the wrong place. But no, I'm fine. The red car is entering the exit ramp! Immediately, I change lanes. There are now three exit lanes. Once out of harm's way, I begin to beep my horn as they do in Barcelona, when the football (soccer) team has just won the World Cup. By this time, the car has passed me, heedless of my warning. I continue on my way as there is no place to park safely on this roadway.

I see this event as a metaphor for my life. I try to be easy going, grateful for the blessings I enjoy. When something happens to threaten me, I quickly snap into gear, plan an escape route and attempt to right the situation. This month, January again, I am faced with my husband Bob being constantly with me, not allowing me any breathing space. When we are in a store, he wants to shop elsewhere and I must monitor his perambulation instead of concentrating on what I need to purchase. He places unnecessary items in the cart. He cannot choose the correct size of something he wants to purchase. This week it was a pair of furry slippers. I had to stop, find a place for him to try the slippers on, to see that they were too small, direct him again to the spot where he found the slippers, and offer him the correct size. Now he no longer wants slippers, "I have perfectly good ones at home," he says. *Right on. Sometimes he snaps right into gear.*

We have not been receiving mail at our Arizona address, although we have now been here for two months. The first time I complain, the regular mail carrier blames the substitute driver. At the post office, the clerk reports "computer error" as she clicks an order into her computer. "It should be fine now." We begin to receive our forwarded mail, but not local mail. Bills are returned to the sender, "Addressee unknown," or "Moved, left no forwarding address." I return to the post office. The supervisor is called. "It seems that there is an overriding "permanent move" on your account instead of a "temporary move," he says flippantly, "It should be all right now." That was one week ago. Yesterday, I put in another appearance at the "blue door" where the supervisors reside. A different supervisor explains, "Everything is in place now. It might take a while."

"How much longer?" I want to know.

"Maybe a week, maybe two," she replies.

So what bothers me is my impotence in every situation I am facing, not only at the post office, but caregiving for a spouse with Alzheimer's disease. Just like at the post office, when reminded, everyone does what is supposed to be done, and the system takes its time complying. I do what I can and Bob's brain throws a monkey wrench into my plans. When he buys shirts, as he did on Tuesday when there were five shirts in Kohl's department store he could not live without, I am patient and compliant. One person recommended I return the excess items that he purchases, but Bob removes all the tags from his purchases immediately on our arrival home, so that solution won't work either. There are 76 shirts in Bob's Arizona closet, all purchased here during the past three winters.

But now all he wants are knives and scissors, which he sharpens in his garage workshop. So far Bob is safely working with his knives and scissors, although I find them in various places in the kitchen drawers. The problem remains Bob's agitation, which may erupt at any time. "If he cuts off his finger," said the social worker from the Alzheimer Institute, "that would be awful. But if he injures you, that would be tragic, for who would take care of him then, or of you, assuming your survival?"

The social worker told a story of a client who was herself a midwife. Her son reassured his father that he was safe, although the father complained of his wife's agitated states. One day, the son returned home to find his father stabbed and left to bleed out. "Fortunately," said the social worker, "he survived. But what if no one had come in time?" She told me, "Phyllis, you are in danger. My advice to you is to place your husband in a day care program where he could develop other interests, be social and reduce somewhat his dependency on you."

Okay, the red car is approaching. Step one, my first instinct is my safety. I reduce the numbers of knives in the kitchen. I hide some and I give them to my son Steve to remove from the house every time he visits. Steve presents me with a serrated-edged plastic knife that could not hurt me, but cuts bread and salad nicely. Never before have I used a plastic knife except for picnics.

For his safety and my sanity, I try to avoid shopping with Bob. As he does not like me to hire caregivers, I have hired a home health agency to provide a housekeeper one day each week for four hours instead of my usual cleaning service. Step two, I make a plan. The plan doesn't work great, as the agency sends different people each week, who don't know where anything is, and my free time is reduced by having to explain the cleaning procedures, equipment and details. The idea was that Bob would get used to one person being here, whose time I could expand when I need to be out of the house for more than a few hours at a time. After a few weeks this plan breaks down. The women report back to the agency that they were trained to be caregivers, not cleaners, and they refuse to work.

Step three; I begin to research adult day care placements. I go to visit two centers and I speak with the workers. I examine the facility, stay for an activity and leave. I feel so terrible each time I depart; I remember my mother at the Adult Day Care Center at Daughters of Israel in West Orange, NJ. The first time my sister Sharyn and I took my mother to the facility it was for an evaluation by the Alzheimer Diagnostic team. We thought then, that our mother was more capable than the other attendees. A few months later, she fit in nicely.

So now I feel that Bob would fit in nicely, but that his awareness of his memory and thinking losses is so great that he will be angry with me for placing him in a facility, no matter how nice it is. Would I exchange a few hours of respite for a return of the agitated angry man? I am afraid. I agree to bring Bob to the Arbor Rose Adult Day Club for a visit. He will be taken care of on Friday afternoon from 2:00 to 3:30 while I attend their twice monthly caregiver's support group. The visit goes well; when I leave the meeting room, Bob is quietly sitting in the library in a leather wing chair reading a book from their library. "Hi, Hon," I say as I put my hand on his shoulder, "What are you reading?" He shows me the book, "I found it here on the shelf," he says.

"Good, I'll be back in a minute; I have to visit the ladies' room." Bob sits quietly reading.

When I return, he asks, "Where are we going now?"

"We're going to the fruit stand, okay?" I explain. Bob is willing to follow me and we leave. Neither of us mentions the visit that day or ever. I do know that Bob was simply waiting for me to be finished, as he waits for me at the beauty parlor, or at a committee meeting that I attend in the evening at the synagogue.

225

On Monday, we go out for lunch and after that I bring him to Arbor Rose, now called "the clubhouse" by me in order to acquaint Bob with the facility which indeed resembles an active adult clubhouse. There's a pool table, a section for snacks, the library, an exercise corner, a television room with recliner seats, a beauty parlor, nice grassy grounds surrounded by a white picket fence. I tell Bob I am leaving for a while but I will be back and, as I have been advised, I leave.

Walking to the car, I feel free and guilty. Would I feel better if I were going to work? There is nowhere I have to be, nothing I have planned to do. I accomplish my errands quickly without having to wait for Bob, who walks slowly and gets distracted by sights and sounds. I go to the bank, where I can take my time, not worrying what Bob will decide to ask or do. I fill the gas tank, not having to allow Bob to hold the hose while I do the gas pump purchase. *Don't get too used to this yet, Phyllis, it may not work.*

When I return, Katie, the worker who greeted us earlier, sees me at the entrance and waves me not to enter. She meets me in the foyer, explaining, "Your husband is sitting at the other side of this wall. He said he was hungry, so we're getting him a snack. Can we talk here?"

What is she going to tell me? I feel like the nursery school child's mother, waiting for a behavior report.

"How did it go?" I begin anxiously.

"Well, the first hour, he walked around, checking us out. The larger group was playing bingo in the all-purpose room, but that was too much for him, so he stayed away from there. Then for the next two hours, he kept asking for you. When I said you had errands to run, shopping to do, he asked why he couldn't go with you. He said at one point that you were abandoning him. He wouldn't do anything dangerous, would he?"

"No, of course not," I reassured her. I do want to bring him back here.

When I entered the café area, Bob had finished his lemon meringue pie, but he was still seated at a long table. Two other men were also seated at the table. "How was the pie, dear?" I asked in greeting.

"Not good," he replied, picked up his book and some papers, and was ready to leave.

"Sorry, sweetheart, you'll have to leave the library book here. You can read it again when you come back," I explained.

"I'm not coming back," said Bob as he placed the book back on the table.

He followed me from the building, asking, "Where are were going now?"

"To the mall to replace your torn watch strap," I say cheerfully, and off we go.

The next day we get a chest x-ray as part of the admission process to the day care center and tomorrow we will see the physician to complete the application process. Today I am looking forward to bringing Bob to the clubhouse, but he sleeps all morning and doesn't get dressed until 2 p.m. So we will try again on Friday.

36 – Was This a Constructive Day?

Arizona, February 2011

What did I do today? It is 7 p.m. and the day began at the gym at 8:15 a.m. I decide to take a kick boxing/step class but I walk out, too fatigued after a half hour to do the fast-paced stepping. I come straight home; Bob is still dressed in his pajamas, so I file some papers, respond to email. Two hours disappear before Bob comes to find me.

"I need help in the kitchen," he says. I follow him and he continues,

"I want to make one of these egg things, but I can't remember how to do it. I have the pan; do I need the larger one or the smaller one? I have the box of eggs; do I use one egg or two? I put olive oil in the pan, but now I don't know what to do."

He is heartbroken. Quietly I take out a bowl and a fork, break the eggs and hand him the fork.

"Mix these together, Bob, and then we'll fry them in the pan you prepared."

Bob mixes the eggs and watches as the pan heats, and then stands waiting for more instructions.

"Pour the egg mixture into the pan now and watch it cook," I add.

I take the sharp cheddar cheese from the refrigerator and cut four small squares, placing them on the cutting board near the range. As the eggs set up, Bob remembers to lift the edge of the omelet to let the looser material flow beneath the set boundaries. Then he sees the cheese.

"Did I cut that up?" he wonders.

"No, I did," I mention.

"Good," he says, "When these are almost done, I'll add the cheese and turn it in half."

Maybe it is coming back. Will he remember to do what he just said?

Sadly, he does not. He wanders away from the range to get a plate, to wash the fork he just used, and to rinse out the bowl, concentrating now on cleaning. I quietly finish the omelet.

Bob then comes over next to me and says, "It is so sad. I have forgotten how to make one of these things. I haven't made one in a while, that's why I forgot."

He's trying to find a reason. This is so sad.

"I know. But luckily you have me here, and we are a great team. We fixed it together."

Okay, now it's close to 1 p.m. I haven't had my shower, although Bob is now dressed. I sort some laundry; get cleaned up while Bob is napping on his comfortable chair in the living room. Back at the computer, I avoid tackling the next chapter of my book, revising instead chapters I have written more recently.

By three, Bob is awake, and asking, "Did we take pictures when we were in Russia?"

"We sure did," I answer happily. Bob is talking to me, remembering a trip.

"Where are we now?" Bob wants to know.

"We're in Arizona," I answer, knowing the question.

"Where are they? Did you bring the books?"

229

"Actually the Russia trip isn't in a book, it is on the computer. Come with me and I'll let you see all of our Russia pictures." We spend the better part of the next hour with Bob looking at our pictures.

"I remember that," he says, pointing at a gazebo, known as the Aviary on the grounds of Tsar Alexander's summer palace outside of St. Petersburg. "It's in a park."

"That's right. We spent the whole day there. There are Sarah and George," I add hopefully. Bob makes no comment, but he continues watching the slide show.

Bob is tiring of this activity because I can see his attention is wandering, so I suggest we watch the pictures again later. Bob staggers slightly as he swivels the chair and stands up.

"I got dizzy getting out of that turning chair," he says. "I'm tired, where are we now?" as he looks left and right in our front hall, "I have to go pee."

"We're in Arizona. Which bathroom would you like to use?"

"There's one right over there. I'll use that one," he says seriously and he walks confidently around the corner.

A few minutes later, he enters the kitchen and I ask, "Would you like a cup of tea and a doughnut? Maybe you're hungry." He already had a nap. But no, Bob returns to his favorite chair and sleeps from 4:09 to 5:15 p.m., when I start to prepare dinner.

Now dinner is finished, Bob is folding the clean clothes. I did get a lot of filing done as Bob was watching the slide show. Maybe it wasn't such a waste of a day after all.

37 – Delusions and Hallucinations

Arizona, February 2011

I saw the film "The Black Swan" last evening, after returning from an Alzheimer support group in the afternoon, where the topic concerned hallucinations and delusions experienced by demented loved ones. The leader suggested the group watch the film "Iris" which portrays Iris Murdoch's visual hallucinations as she and her now elderly husband bathe in the river. She "sees" herself and her spouse as they were then, young and vibrant, and is frightened when she then sees her husband as he is in reality.

The Alzheimer Association defines delusions as "false beliefs" and hallucinations as "distortions in a person's perception of reality." They continue, "Hallucinations may be sensory experiences in which a person sees, hears, smells, tastes or feels something that is not there." It is important for us caregivers to know that delusions and hallucinations can occur with some frequency in persons with dementia and we need to deal with our reactions to these events. In order to help us cope, an experience on film can show us something about how our loved ones see the world. Natalie Portman in the film "The Black Swan" shows her character's inability to distinguish fact from fiction, what she perceives is seen as reality and she *acts* on what she perceives. That's the scary part for me.

"Do you smell the perfume in the air?" Bob some-times asks, or he states, "Something in this house smells awful," and he empties the trash. Both events are unique to his perception. I have smelled nothing out of the ordinary.

All well and good. Nothing dangerous here, right?

He has also been very angry with birds for landing on our patio, or for building nests on our house, and extremely upset if a fly enters our home. He hoses the birds and using his cloth napkin, swooshes at the fly in an aggressive-feeling way. He is acting on the perceived threat he is experiencing from the birds and the fly. I know we are in no danger from either, but he does not.

Bob also perceives any absence of mine over two hours in duration as abandonment. Before I leave I write him a note, I show Bob the note and place it at his place at the dining table. The note details the day, the time I depart and the time I will return, and indicates my des-tination and lists my cell phone number. He has never called me. When I return, he does not greet me or smile. He seems angry with me.

When I am home, Bob looks to see me every ten minutes or so, just checking to make sure I am here. If there is a cleaning person in the house, he asks, "Where's Phyllis?" in an angry tone, when he sees her and not me in a room.

He does not smile or engage me in conversation when he "discovers" me, usually in my office, but even in the bathroom. Sometimes he acts so surprised when he encounters me in the house, either reentering from putting something outside in the trash bin, or exiting the laundry room as he is walking by. "Oh, here you are." he exclaims. "I didn't know you were here."

Where did you think I was? I am stuck here with you 24/7.

I live afraid. What if my beloved sweet husband acts on his angry feelings toward me in a hostile way? Bob has obsessions. Last year he was obsessed with purchasing shirts, colorful, short-sleeved shirts we used to call Hawaiian shirts. This winter, he will no longer go with a companion anywhere, wanting only to go with me. I don't go to thrift stores. When he accompanies me to a department store, he still sometimes sees shirts and insists on buying them. I don't stop him. Now he only wants to buy knives and scissors. Even in Walgreens's, the pharmacy, Bob finds packages of scissors.

"Only five dollars," he says, "what a bargain. I can't pass these up."

In Costco he buys knives. Even in the supermarket, he finds the section where knives are sold. I was advised to return these unwanted purchases, but Bob holds the package in his lap during the ride home. He takes the wrapping off as soon as we enter the house and adds this new possession to his collections. The problem is that Bob continually sharpens these knives and scissors. They become so sharp that is not safe for me to handle them; I do need some knives for cooking. Knowing how to sharpen knives makes Bob feel useful as well as competent. So does cleaning and sorting his tools. He is so proud of how clean he keeps his workshop and how sharp he hones his tools. When I engage Bob in cutting vegetables for dinner and preparing the salad, he reminds me to be careful not to cut myself on the sharp edges. He washes the knives by hand, not trusting them to the dishwasher which could endanger the glue which bonds the knife to the shaft. This is not new behavior; we've had this discussion for years.

What am I going to do? Bob needs other activities; he needs companionship. When I invite friends for dinner, at home or in a restaurant, Bob does not participate. He does not want a companion, hired to be with him. He does not want to return to the Day Club. My daughter does not want young Grant to be here if Grandpa is going to be angry; no one chooses to be in our company. All of my plans to have a life for myself are in ruin. I am back being a prisoner.

38 – Put That Knife Away

Arizona, February 2011

"Put that knife away! I am afraid of you!" screams my husband as I carve the roasted chicken for our Friday night dinner.

"I have a knife too," he continues as he pulls a long bread knife from behind his back and brandishes it in front of him as if he has just unsheathed a sword.

My thoughts had been far from here, remembering the candles, the challah and the wine that welcomed the Sabbath in our home and at my parents' home. I look up, dazed but mellow.

"Okay," I say quietly, "I'll make a deal with you. I'll put the carving knife down, and you put the bread knife down."

"No, I don't have to. You're not the boss of me. I'm the boss and you better know it."

Bob is standing at the other end of our long dining table, at least six feet from me. Our dining table is set for two, with a clean green cloth and matching napkins; my grandmother's Bavarian porcelain fruit bowl sitting at the center. It is white with a gold rim, the center is painted with pictures of fruit; an apple, a pear and some strawberries, none of which can now be seen, as the bowl is filled to the brim with apples, pears and bananas. I am standing at the far end near Bob's seat at the head of the table. I sit to his left, nearer to the range and oven, and close enough to the island to place or retrieve platters.

I am not afraid for my safety, but he sounds so enraged I am afraid for his control. He walks to the table, picks up his cloth napkin, wraps the knife in it and walks into our bedroom. I believe he is going to hide the knife, now that his scare tactic has not frightened me, and he is therefore a bit less agitated himself. I follow him discreetly, remaining by the double-door entrance to the bedroom.

"Why are you following me?" Bob wants to know.

"Because if you are hiding the knife, I have to know where it is, so I can find it later," I answer truthfully. Bob turns, holding the covered knife and walks past me, heading toward his "office." I do not follow. I'll worry about the knife some other time. I wait a while, and call him in to dinner.

"I'm not eating. I'm not hungry. I still don't trust you," he says from his room.

So I package the cut-up chicken, place it in a Pyrex dish, cover it with tin foil; I package the crisp green asparagus as well, as if they were leftovers and store them and the baked potato in the refrigerator. I may be calm on the outside, but my insides are upset and my nerves are raw.

What has led up to this frightening event? Why is Bob so paranoid now? I will recount this difficult day. I left Bob at the Arbor Rose Day Center this morning for the first time since he attended with Irving last Friday, a week ago. When he entered, it was about 11 a.m. He walked back into the center accompanied by an aide, who placed a name tag on his chest, put her hand on his shoulder and spoke kindly to him, hoping to involve him in the music therapy activity in progress. I was still speaking with the staff about forms when he returned to the desk and said he did not want to be there.

"Bob, do you like coffee? Would you like to sit in the café and have coffee and talk this over with your wife?" asks Katy. She motions to another worker, probably unfortunately named Steve, to bring two mugs of coffee to the table, meanwhile asking Bob, "Do you take cream and sugar in your coffee?"

Bob is not turning toward the coffee discussion. He is yelling, "Look what she is doing to me. She is spending all my money, money that my children should get, not her children." Another worker comes over to where I am seated at the table and whispers, "You don't have to listen to this. We'll take care of it. Come, I'll show you another way out."

So, feeling guilty and tense, I leave for my respite time. I have not much respite. I am worried the whole afternoon that someone will telephone me and tell me to come to remove my husband from the site. When they don't call to tell me to pick my husband up, I am afraid I never left my cell phone number with Arbor Rose and that the office is calling me at home. So I return home. No phone messages there either. I phone Arbor Rose to ask how the day is going.

"Pretty good," Josie, the telephone receptionist answers, "He settled down after our nurse talked with him. He ate lunch, not when all the others ate, but later. So I think it is going all right for the first day. Don't worry."

"I think I'll come get him now," I answer.

When I arrive at the center, it is 3:00 p.m. I see Bob seated in the café, at a table at which several other old men are seated. None has a smile; no one is speaking. I enter, walk up to Bob and say, "Hi, Hon, are you ready to come home?" Bob is silent. He won't make eye contact with me. A tall, lean, smiling man walks over and introduces himself to me. "Hello, Phyllis," he says, extending his right hand, "I'm Darcy, the nurse in charge. I am also a part-owner of Arbor Rose Day Care Center."

"Hi Darcy," I reply. "We've spoken on the telephone. I am glad to meet you. How did the day go?"

Darcy looks at Bob, but speaks to me. "I think it went well for the first day. Bob settled in and I think he had a good time."

Then he says to Bob, "Your wife is here. It's time to go home."

"Where's home? Which home? Where are we going? With her?" Bob asks, pointing his chin at me. Darcy turns to me and asks where we live. I understand my husband is disoriented. He has no idea what state he is in. "Arizona, Bob. We're going to our Arizona house."

"And who lives there with us?"

"No one, just us. Let's go. I need to fill the tank with gas."

I turn to leave. Staff members call out "Goodbye" to Bob, saying "See you on Monday," or "Have a nice weekend."

Bob does not reply, but follows me out of the center and to the car, where he enters the back seat. Is this because when Irving was here, Bob often let his brother have the better view from the front seat or is he angry with me? I don't know. It doesn't matter. We leave. At the gas station, Bob does not exit the car, lets me fill up the tank by myself. Usually he wants to participate. I say nothing. The process is faster when I do it alone. We go to the market. Bob follows me like a dog, quietly. I shop. He adds nothing to the cart, says nothing. We pay and walk out. He unloads the groceries from the cart into the trunk of the car, and then sits in the back seat again. This time I know he is upset with me. Saying nothing myself, we return home and Bob unloads the groceries from the trunk, leaving them on the counter. I finish unpacking the groceries and begin to prepare dinner. Noticing that it is very quiet in the house, I turn on the radio to the classical music station and go in search of Bob. I find him asleep in the guest bedroom. I prepare dinner leisurely, absorbed in my own thoughts. When he comes out with the knife, I am surprised as I thought Bob had been asleep. He must have quietly sneaked into the kitchen behind me to get the knife and to hide it behind his back before speaking to me.

For an hour after Bob goes into his office with the knife, I worry what he is doing, but I am afraid to aggravate him so I do nothing. I am also still shaking and a bit frightened. I cannot manage this psychotic behavior. These incidents are happening too frequently now. There is no way I can organize Bob's life to protect him or me from these outbursts. I prepare a cup of tea and a doughnut for Bob and call him to the table.

"I'm not hungry," he repeats, still in his office. I bring the medications, the tea and a doughnut to his desk.

"That's okay," I answer, "but you still have to take your evening meds. I think you can manage a chocolate-covered doughnut and tea."

Bob sits and I leave the room. After his dessert, Bob undresses and goes to bed, in the guest bedroom. By three in the morning, I sense his presence next to me, where he belongs.

On Saturday and Sunday, it rains, which is unusual for the desert. Most Arizonans carry on with their lives without hats or umbrellas, enjoying the rain. For me, it is an excuse to have a quiet time, recuperating from Friday. My children insist I remove all the knives from the house. First, I remove all the sharp knives, leaving the steak knives and the paring knives. Bob doesn't notice. But on Saturday afternoon, when he sees that the butcher-block knife holder and its contents are missing from the kitchen counter, his anger flares again.

"Where are my knives?" Bob screams. "That is my property. I made that knife holder. You stole it from me. Why? Do you want to give it to Steve? Aren't you even waiting for me to die before you start taking my things?" He goes into his office and slams the door. He remains in his office all afternoon. But aside from some mumbling, I hear no more about the knives, until Sunday.

On Sunday evening Ted and Grant arrive for dinner. Linda and Dave are away celebrating Dave's birthday in Palm Springs and Uncle Ted is minding Grant for the weekend. We finally eat Friday's chicken which I have baked with Chinese sweet and sour sauce and some vegetable broth until the meat falls from the bone. I add broad noodles which have been tossed with chicken gravy, broccoli "trees" which Grant likes, and salad.

During dinner, Eliot, Bob's friend from New Jersey, returns Bob's telephone call and Bob leaves the table to speak with him in private.

After another hour, Bob's son phones and Bob says, "I need to talk to you. Do you have time now to talk to me?"

Bob leaves the room and speaks with his son for a long time. After Ted and Grant leave, Bob is enraged again. *Did he hold in his anger while we entertained guests? How is this possible?* Bob shouts that his son is a lawyer and he will "take care of you. You will have no money; people will throw pennies at you in the street."

By Monday, I am afraid to send him to the day care center again. I am fearful on Tuesday, as well. Bob is quiet, not talking to me, sleeping in the guest bedroom. I spend much of my time on the computer.

Tuesday afternoon, my son Ted stops by. Bob calls him into his room and rails at him against me. He uses foul language, tells Ted awful things he will do to me and Ted is visibly shaken.

"It won't be much longer until Bob will need to be hospitalized," he says. "He is talking about hitting you with a baseball bat, and much worse," he reports.

Ted worked for a psychiatrist for several years so he is familiar with patient behavior. He takes the remaining knives with him when he leaves. But meanwhile we have tickets for 7 p.m. to see a movie. It is part of the Scottsdale Jewish Film Festival. We have seen two films already, the first with Irving, and the second with a group of friends I met at the gym.

I ask Bob, "If you are so angry with me, maybe I'll take Ted with me to see the film. You can stay home by yourself."

"Why can't I go to the movies?" he asks. "I don't have to sit next to you. I don't have to talk to you. I'll just go to the movies." The reverse psychology works; I couldn't leave Bob home alone.

We drive to the theater in silence. Bob chooses his seat in the center of a high row. I sit next to him; he moves over leaving one seat vacant between us. When my friends arrive, they wish to sit with us. Bob refuses to move one seat in either direction, so we have him in the middle and converse around him. He says nothing. He watches the film and he eats his M&M's. After the film, he remains in his seat until everyone else has left the theater. We are waiting in the lobby. Bob does not arrive. I send a theater worker to check the men's room, twice. Both times, he reports the men's room empty. We search the theater and the parking lot until Bob emerges from the men's room. He must have been in a stall, not responding to the queries.

By Wednesday morning, I phone Adele and explain this five day saga. She tells me I have to have some rest from this man.

"Send him to the day care," she orders. "They are trained. They can handle him."

So by 11:00, I am dressed, Bob is dressed and I decide to take Bob to the Arbor Rose Day Center. I look for Bob; I can't find him. He is absolutely not in our house or on our property. I drive the car to search for him. I find him standing in front of a construction site, happily watching a man driving a large piece of machinery, digging a trench for a new home.

I invite him to join me; he doesn't. I turn off the motor and I wait. Fifteen minutes later, Bob decides probably that he has seen enough, and enters the car. I drive to the pharmacy first, purchase what I need, and then I drive to the care center. Katy is standing in the driveway on Bob's side of the car. I open the window.

"Hi, Bob," says Katy. "Are you coming to see us today? Do you want to wait out here with me? I am waiting for the pizza delivery. We're having pizza for lunch."

"It's all right with me," says Bob.

Katy opens the door, unlocks Bob's seat belt for him and helps Bob exit the car.

She waves to me, and says to Bob, "Your wife is going to park the car."

I leave, return home, and make some telephone calls to see if I can get a psychiatric consult before March 16, which is still three weeks away, when we are scheduled for an intake interview at Banner Alzheimer Institute. I am waiting for return calls when Darcy phones.

"Phyllis?" he begins with a questioning voice, "I have an idea I want you to mull over for a while."

"Why, what's happening? Is Bob upset?"

"Not in any way we can't handle. But frankly, I think his medications need some tweaking. We have a relationship with a free-standing hospital. Some of our patients go there for a week to ten days and come back much more manageable and able to live at home for a longer period of time."

"Tell me more," I say.

"It's right here in Phoenix. It's a lovely environment. Bob would get excellent care. Medicare covers it, plus if you have another policy, it helps," Darcy continues. "And we could help you by escorting him there. If I call, it could even happen today, if you want."

"Make the call and see," I decide. A few minutes later, a social worker from the Haven Senior Horizons Hospital phones me.

"Do you have a mental health power of attorney?" the woman asks.

"No," I reply. "My husband was already incompetent when I found out about this draconian Arizona law," I respond.

"Then are you willing to admit him, are you willing to file for guardianship?" she needs to know.

"Let me find out what that entails," I respond.

"Could your husband possibly have a UTI?" she asks. "That can sometimes cause a rage reaction," she adds.

A UTI is a urinary tract infection. Bob had one of those last May. Perhaps a urinary tract infection caused his psychotic break last May. I have seen that he is changing his underpants during the day. I see the left ones all over the place.

"Maybe this is possible," I muse aloud into the phone.

"Why don't you take your husband over to the hospital and see if there is a medical reason for his change in behavior? Then they could send him directly to us and we could deal with the psychiatric issues.

"All right, I will have him medically cleared," I say, "and then we'll know more about what to do."

Darcy permits Katy to accompany us to the hospital, which is just around the block from the day center. All afternoon long as we wait from 1:20 p.m. when we arrive, until 2:42 when we are admitted to an ER room, Bob complains to Katy about me and my children and praises his children, although he no longer remembers their names, except for Adam, and doesn't know where they live. He only knows they went to college, they are not gay or divorced or remarried and they all have jobs. He is very proud of his children.

When he meets a physician's assistant, Avi, he begins anew. He speaks of hurting me violently, curses me and accuses me.

Avi tells me, "There is almost no way this man is going home with you tonight."

The first thing Bob wants to do is urinate. I get the staff to provide a specimen bottle, as this is what we are here to collect. They do, he does, and soon the specimen is misplaced, which we do not find out for quite a while.

They decide to do a CAT scan of Bob's head. Bob is not cooperative with this procedure or with the heparin lock or the blood draw.

They decide to sedate him, which no one asks or tells me about.

They perform their tests, and then come for a urine sample. Bob is too tired to perform. Besides, he hasn't had anything to eat or drink except for a small applesauce. Katy tells me he didn't eat the pizza for lunch, either. All he had was a cup of coffee and a brownie.

They catheterize him to obtain the sample. The staff report to me they find no medical reason for his rage behavior.

By now it is close to 10 p.m. I am tired. I am not very nice when I am tired. I say to the charge nurse, "We are going home. Please order a wheelchair and have someone help me get this sleeping man to my car."

"I'll have to advise the PA (physician's assistant)," he adds. The woman who replaced Avi at 7 p.m. when his shift terminated has not seen Bob or me at all. Now she walks up, introduces herself and suggests we wait for the psychiatrist.

"Sorry, but no," I respond. "This man is asleep. He cannot be interviewed. The psychiatrist will be limited to reading the notes from today. He will see how violent my husband's language was and he will refer him to a psychiatric hospital since he will not be able to admit him to this facility."

"Why don't you go home and rest and your husband can remain here in the ER until he sleeps it off." she offers.

"No, thank you, I am not leaving him here. What if he wakes up disoriented, and becomes enraged without me here? He will definitely end up in a locked ward somewhere," I respond.

"Let me at least phone the on-call psychiatrist?" she asks.

"Okay, but ask him or her for a prescription. The Seroquel XR 300 mg is not holding him."

"I didn't know he was on Seroquel 300 mg XL. What else is he taking? We have no record of his medications."

"No one asked me," I added, irritated with her and this lengthy invasive process.

"Let's rectify that," she continues, but she doesn't. She waits probably for a return phone call from the physician and returns, saying,

"The doctor said I could write the prescription. You can go home if you think you will be safe."

If he were your spouse what would you do?

39 – The Psychiatric Hospital

Arizona, February 2011

On Thursday we go together to the pharmacy to fill the new prescription. Breakfast, shower and dressing have all gone smoothly. Bob slept in our bed, rolled over for hugs and a backrub at 7 a.m. and I am relaxing. The experience from yesterday seems to be forgotten, and he is no longer angry with me. We will begin the new medication, 0.5 mg Risperidone tomorrow, as Bob already took his Seroquel at breakfast.

The morning goes by smoothly, but Bob cannot settle. He doesn't know what to do. He is not able to concentrate on either of the two magazines, "Popular Mechanics" and "Popular Science" that we purchased at the pharmacy as we waited for the medication. I call Linda and ask her to meet us at Bob's favorite restaurant, The Village Inn, for a late lunch – just for an activity.

We return home and Bob sits on his chair and dozes. All of a sudden, he pops up, asking for his brother's telephone number. I dial and he reaches his brother's answer machine. Bob is distressed that his immediate desire cannot be fulfilled. "Why doesn't my brother answer his telephone? Where is he?"

When Irving returns Bob's call, he takes the telephone outside. I listen on the extension. Bob is complaining to Irving, "She sends me to this place where there are all these old people. They don't talk, they're all stupid. I don't want to go there."

Later, I tell Bob, "You don't have to go to the club-house if you don't want to. Irving went with you last week and he thought it would be a good place for you to be, so you would have something to do. Sometimes," I continue, "I have to go places where you don't want to be, so either you are at the clubhouse or I hire someone to stay home with you. That's your choice."

"Why can't I go with you?" Bob asks.

"Well, you didn't like going with me to the syna-gogue last week. You sat in the library, but you got bored and interrupted the meeting. That made every-one uncomfortable."

"Okay, I'll stay home," Bob says.

"Great, I'll call the agency and set up a schedule." I call Visiting Angels Home Care Agency and set up a meeting for Monday at 10 a.m.

Then Bob says, "Isn't there a doctor I could see to see if they can fix what's wrong with me?"

I answer, "Yes, there is. I just spoke to someone rec ommended by Darcy at the clubhouse. Do you want to talk with her?"

"Sure," Bob says and I phone Terry, the social work-er at Haven Senior Horizons hospital.

Bob speaks with Terry, who explains the in-patient process and how they look at all the medicines Bob takes to see which ones are good for him and which ones might need to be changed.

"I think I need that," Bob says as he hands the tele-phone to me.

"It looks like you had a moment of lucidity there," Terry tells me. "But I'm sure your husband will not remember agreeing as he just did. You will have to sign him in. He is not competent to sign himself in."

I prepare dinner. Bob refuses to eat, refuses to take his medicines.

"I think you're trying to poison me," he says.

The moment of lucidity is gone.

On Friday, we begin the new medication. Bob is once again sweet and compliant in the morning. He eats breakfast at 7:15 a.m. He spends his time in the garage or in his room. I stay home doing laundry. Bob helps me fold the clean dry clothes. Bob eats the lunch I prepare, which is mushroom barley soup and a bologna sandwich; he takes the 1:15 p.m. Risperidone pill with a cup of tea and a half of a chocolate doughnut and places the dirty dishes in the dishwasher when he is finished. Perfect!

My emotions fluctuate along with Bob's actions. I am thrilled when he complies and is pleasant; devastated each time he acts out. I cannot find any one attitude of my own that works consistently. Sometimes he feels I am condescending, sometimes he feels I am bossy, but he never appreciates me anymore. I cannot predict his moods anymore. I am frightened and uncomfortable waiting to see his reactions each ten minutes of the day.

We seem to have a new pattern here as Bob is once again frightened at dinner time and refuses to eat or to take his evening medications.

He curses at me and then he says, "I'll take them in the morning. I don't trust you."

By 9 p.m. he is asleep in the guest bedroom. My children ask me to lock my bedroom door. I don't want to do so, as I need to be alert if Bob wakes up during the night and needs my help. But I do. The lock is merely one that can be opened with a pin inserted into the hole.

In the morning I hear Bob try the door. When he sees it is locked, he goes away, so I take my shower. As I stand wrapped in my bath towel, Bob appears smiling, in the bathroom. He has a thin awl in his hand with which he has successfully opened the door.

"I'll be next when you're done," he says calmly as he walks out of the bathroom.

I say nothing. I am amazed at his successful completion of a self-directed action and of course, now I have to get a real lock on this door if I want to be safe. Once someone comes after you with a knife, it is only a matter of time until he does it again.

After breakfast, Bob takes a shower, but it is too quiet, so I check. He is asleep in our bed, under the bedspread.

"What's the matter?" I ask.

"I'm dizzy," he answers sleepily. He sleeps for an hour and I check again.

Bob is dressed, seated on his chair in our room, dozing.

"What's happening, Bob?" I ask.

"I'm dizzy," Bob answers.

"Well, maybe we should go to the hospital and get your medications checked. The new medication must be making you dizzy. You're not usually dizzy in the morning. You ate well, you slept well."

I am concerned. This is a powerful medication. I need my husband to be safe. I call my daughter and tell her I need help. She calls my younger son, Ted, to babysit for Grant. Dave is exercising at the gym, so we plan for Linda and Dave to accompany me and Bob to the hospital at noon.

By noon, Bob again refuses to eat the grilled cheese sandwich I prepare. I don't give him any more medication. Dave is concerned about his wife's safety and he and my son Ted arrive to escort Bob to the hospital. Ted explains the situation to Bob." Come with us in Dave's car. We're going to let you speak with someone about the problems you're having with Mom."

Bob goes with the two men willingly. I hide in another part of the house, so he doesn't see me.

I phone Steve and we drive to the hospital in my car. We are met by the intake worker Madrassa, not Terry, as she's not working today. She escorts us to her office in the administration wing of the hospital, away from the locked unit. The three men wait alone in the consultation room, as Bob is not permitted to enter the unit until I have completed the admission forms.

As they wait, Bob gets agitated again and says, "That bitch of a wife of mine took all my knives, but she didn't get this one," and he removes his pocket knife from his jeans pocket and opens it, brandishing it as if he wanted to slice someone with it.

Ted, who reported this scene to me afterwards said, "What a neat-looking knife. Let me hold it," and he walked out of the unit with the knife.

Meanwhile Bob forgets who Dave and Ted are. He thinks they work for the hospital.

When Dave walks out to use the facilities and then returns, Bob says, "I know you. You're the tall one."

A nurse arrives to lead Bob into the unit and the guys leave to drive home. Steve and I complete the assessment forms and we leave the hospital without seeing Bob, who will be in the hospital for ten to fourteen days.

40 – Agida

Arizona, March 2011

The American-Italian slang word for that awful feeling in the pit of my stomach when I am upset describes how I am feeling better than any English, French or German word I know. Leaving Bob in the hospital was one of the most difficult tasks I have ever had to do. I drop Steve off at his house, so I return to an empty house, alone, wondering if Bob will ever be here again. All of my plans for having Bob live his life in the comfort of his own home, among his own belongings, his garden, his books, his workshop would be lost. Perhaps the doctors will be able to stabilize him on medications and send him home to me in two weeks.

Meanwhile, I have to rest. I am exhausted. Sunday goes by in a blur. I worry that I admitted Bob to the psychiatric unit on the weekend. No psychiatrist will see him until Monday. He will be so confused. I worry that he will forget me. I worry if I sent the right clothing; I am a mess. I don't want to see anyone or do anything. I just need to sit home; I can't concentrate on anything anyway.

Monday morning I phone the unit. A behavioral tech answers the telephone and as we are speaking, Bob walks up to her desk. I hear him ask if the name on the chart he sees is his doctor.

The woman answers, "That says your name."

He repeats his question three times. She answers the same way patiently each time.

Then she says, "Why don't you go to the television room across the hall and wait for the doctor in there?"

"Should I look for him there?" Bob asks.

"No, she answers, "I'll look for him and I'll come to get you in a minute."

So I know he is calm, he is walking around, and of course, he is also confused. The social worker returns my call later in the day. She says the psychiatrist removed all of his medications this morning and left only the Risperidone, but that Bob is no longer dizzy. She explains that the medication often makes the person dizzy when it is first administered. She says Bob has attended one group activity and remained in the room with the group for thirty minutes, which she felt was good. She had nothing more to report, said I should wait a few days before phoning him and that she would phone me on Wednesday.

I email his children that their father has been hospitalized and I get a vituperative response from Adam, as well as a request from Lauren to speak with the hospital. I send her the telephone number and leave a message for Andrea the social worker to accept their calls. I walk two miles on the indoor track with a friend on Monday morning before we go to a Weight Watcher's meeting.

I've lost five pounds, without really trying, and then we shop at the health food store for meals that are microwavable and low in points. I return to the exercise class for the first time in a week on Tuesday before purchasing new locks for my office door and for our bedroom door. These locks will need to be opened with a key, not with a thin sharp tool. Steve is happy to install the locks for me because he is afraid Bob will hurt me with a knife while I am asleep.

Wednesday morning, I speak with my friend Adele who is a social worker in New York. She orders me to take care of myself during this vacation, not to worry in advance about what might be or might not be. Time will tell. "Relax," she says, "eat well, sleep, read a light novel, watch a movie."

She is in Florida this week, following her own advice. Adele has been very stressed after a short visit to North Carolina to visit her recently divorced daughter and her three young granddaughters Traveling by bus on an all-night trip twice within one week was too much for her. She has not been able to enjoy her vacation until today, and tomorrow she returns to winter weather and to work in New York. I know how she feels.

41 – Seven to Ten Days

Arizona, March 2011

I feel I had no choice but to hospitalize my husband, yet I feel so sorry that I needed to take this step. I hope the doctors will remove all medications to see if some chemical he is ingesting is causing the agitation, paranoia and delusional thinking we have all experienced.

Then, after observing him, I hope the doctors will prescribe medications which will keep him calm. I know the Risperidone is a good medication for these symptoms; I have seen it work with patients in my practice, but the dosage has to be titrated properly which we were naturally unable to do.

The social worker informs me that the physician has indeed ordered that all medication be suspended except for diabetes and heart (cholesterol) medication. An observation period will begin and Risperidone in a smaller dose will be added slowly. The team which met this Monday will meet again next Monday and a discharge plan will be drawn. I am requested not to visit; she will supervise a telephone visit on Thursday and we will proceed from there.

I feel reassured; Andrea repeats the same message many times a day, every day and every week. This hospital has only 30 beds; the patients are all seniors. I feel they know what they are doing. I will wait and be patient.

On Thursday, I receive a telephone message from Dr. O., the psychiatrist, who phoned at 9:12, while I was at the gym. Try as I might, I am unable to reach him by telephone at the number he left. The answer machine relates the doctor's private practice address. It is only two miles from our home. The voice on the answering machine states that office hours begin at 11:30 a.m. on Tuesdays, Wednesdays and Thursdays.

I phone my son Ted, who drives with me to the doctor's office to see if he will ask me his questions before beginning his office hours. We wait for a half hour. No secretary or physician appear until 11:45. We are told the doctor is solidly booked for the three hours he will be in the office. If we want to wait, he may be able to see us if a patient is late for an appointment. Several patients arrive for their fifteen minute medication appointments and we leave, disappointed. We now have to wait until Monday to find out what information the doctor wanted to convey or what questions he wanted to ask.

Meanwhile, on Thursday afternoon at 2:30, Andrea phones. "Hi Phyllis, it's Andrea calling," she begins, "I have Bob here with me to talk to you."

"Hi Andrea, Hi Bob," I say. I hear Andrea talking to Bob, "No, just leave the telephone there. You will be able to hear her. Just sit back and talk to Phyllis."

"Phyllis, Phyllis, how did you find me? I miss you. I haven't held you in days." Bob is in tears, he is so happy to hear my voice. I have tears in my eyes as well, as I am always happy when my husband is happy with me. *See, the hospital knows what it is doing. Bob will be better.*

"Hi sweetheart, I miss you too. Would you like me to come to visit you?"

"Yes, yes, I want to hug you. I don't even have to touch you. Just seeing you will be good enough for me." Bob continues, "I love you. You know I love you and I want to be with you."

I promise to visit Bob in the hospital the following afternoon, with Andrea supervising the visit.

I arrive at the hospital precisely at three, when the visiting hour begins. I am nervous, as I always am when visiting a locked psychiatric ward. I have visited patients of mine who were adolescents and I've conducted evaluations and therapy sessions in locked psychiatric wards. It is not a comfortable feeling either for me to be locked in with a patient in a confined space or for me to hear how much the patient wants to leave the hospital when I am not able to grant that wish.

I wait at the entry for Andrea to be summoned. After fifteen minutes, another family is admitted to the unit and I walk in, also. I sign the visitor's book and look around me.

There are very old people, men and women, watching a new flat-screen, large size television set, seated in leather armchairs in an open room to my right. In front of me is a glassed-in room with tables and chairs. This room is both the activities room and the dining room, and several people are seated in chairs, but not Bob. I walk to my left, pass the consultation room and arrive at the nurse's station. I introduce myself and I'm asked to wait in the consultation room until Andrea has completed a telephone call. I wait. I unpack the grapes and the magazines I have brought with me. I actually see Bob walk past the room in which I am sitting, but I do not call out to him as he has not seen me. He looks good; he is wearing a clean blue plaid shirt with the long sleeves rolled up and khakis. I did not pack a pair of khakis and he was wearing jeans when he arrived at the hospital last Friday. He is wearing his khaki-colored cap and seems to be taking a walk around the floor. He looks much younger than the other patients I have seen.

Andrea arrives and tells me the physicians have decreased the Risperidone and added Depakote sprinkles to Bob's medication regimen, due to irritability and that Bob is calmer now. I see Bob walk past the consultation room again, and I rise to greet him. He is very happy to see me, hugging me and kissing me with tears running down his face. He paces around the room, opening and closing drawers; he eats some grapes and leafs through the magazines.

"Let me just look at you," he says. "You are my wife," he continues, "and I love to look at you."

Andrea sees that the visit is going well and excuses herself. "Why don't you show your wife your room?" she asks.

Bob remembers where his room is and shows me his belongings which are all laid out on one of the two beds. The drawers are empty. I see the clothing is labeled 'Robert L', but that some clothing is labeled 'Bill S'. I see no sign of a roommate, so I take the clothing out to the nurses' station.

"That's okay," the nurse answers, "We'll take care of it. That happens all the time."

When I reenter Bob's room, he suggests, "I could move this other bed over and you could stay here with me."

Some parts of Bob are still functioning, I see. We visit for an hour and then the nurse tells me to leave. It is time for medications and then dinner. I walk Bob to the dining room and I leave with a positive attitude as well as a hug and a kiss goodbye, promising to return soon.

Okay, I need one more test before I welcome Bob home.

I invite Steve to join me on Sunday to visit Bob. If, I think, Bob is friendly to Steve as well as to me, and if he can tolerate both of us together, then I will be satisfied that the medications are working and that Bob is ready to come home.

The visit goes so well, Bob hugs Steve as well as me; he talks about all the hospital procedures, the EKG, the urine collection, the finger sticks to test for glucose levels. He is relevant, coherent and friendly. He is wearing someone else's new sneakers. The clothing is again on the bed but belongs to John S this time.

We remain until 4:50 p.m. until the charge nurse tells us to leave.

"And besides," she says, "We don't allow cell phones in here."

We have been sharing pictures with Bob, not placing calls, we explain, which calms her.

"But you still have to leave," she says, "You've been here much longer than the visiting hour."

I can't wait for the next day, when the treatment team will meet and decide when Bob can return home.

Steve and I stop at Sports Authority and purchase new sneakers for Bob so he can give back the ones he borrowed.

42 – The Decision

Arizona, March 2011

It is Monday morning. Although I ask to be present at the treatment team meeting I am told I will be patched in by teleconference call instead. I phone Ted and ask him to be at my house by 8:30 a.m., so he can listen as well. I know how hard it is to hear and really listen to news that is very emotional. I need an objective person to write notes and fill me in on what I may miss.

The phone rings at 8:20 a.m. Luckily Ted is already here. It is the psychiatrist, Dr. O. He wants to ask me some questions about Bob's history of anxiety and depression before the dementia diagnosis. I share my observations and Bob's medical history. I ask if he is preparing for the treatment team meeting.

"This is your information meeting," he replies. "Our telephone system is not working; I'm calling you from my cell phone." I motion to Ted to pick up the extension phone.

"I will add some Lexapro to your husband's meds," the doctor continues, "as he is very emotional, crying. He is on a lower dose of the Risperidone, 0.25 mg twice a day, rather than the 0.5 mg he was taking, to which we added Depakote sprinkles to manage his agitation. He needs redirection every five minutes. He cannot participate in any group activity for more than a few minutes."

"Thank you, doctor," I say, "I know my husband needed new medications. What is your discharge plan?"

"There is no rush. We will keep him until you find a suitable place for him. Andrea will telephone you later. She knows the places in the area and will be a great help to you in finding the right one."

"He can't come home?" I stutter.

"No, I don't know how you have been managing this long. Your husband is a very sick man. If you don't place him now, I cannot guarantee your safety or his, and he will need to be placed within the next five to seven months in any case. It is much better to place him directly from the hospital."

"What if I hire help to care for him at home?" I try.

"Then you will become a full-time employment manager. There are few people trained to provide the services he needs at home. He needs constant monitoring. It is a full time job. People call in sick. They don't come. Don't do this to yourself. You deserve a life and not to be sick yourself. I cannot guarantee your safety or his if he returns home."

43 – A New Era

Arizona, March 3, 2011

My first reaction, after it sinks into my head that Bob cannot return home, is that I failed. Somehow I am not skillful enough or compassionate enough to deal with Bob's issues. I'm just plain scared and tired from not sleeping through the night. *Maybe I shouldn't have placed him in the hospital. Maybe I should have dealt with the knives differently. Bob's not a violent person, why do I believe the stories of people getting stabbed while they sleep?* These feelings keep me awake and intrude often during my day, even as my rational self knows I can't keep the promise I made to myself and to Bob that he remain home in our lovely, handicap-accessible house until the end of his days. My second reaction is to do the opposite of what the doctor just said. He said there is no rush, but I need to hurry in order to get Bob out of the hospital as soon as possible, for my sanity as well as for Bob's comfort. This disorder in my head will continue until I can see what lies ahead for us. Bob has been complaining of daily finger sticks to check his blood sugar, which he does not need. He says they are collecting urine ("someone stands there and watches me pee"), performing EKG's, and then bathing him ("a man who is all dressed washed me in the shower when I am naked"). The sooner I can find a place, the sooner these intrusive procedures will cease.

My third reaction, simultaneous in time, remains my hope that perhaps this move will not be permanent. Maybe, if Bob's behavior is stable or if his memory fails another step and he forgets about being angry, he will be calm and could return home with an aide to help with tasks of daily living. I feel as if this is something I can do. Worrying about this change isn't going to accomplish anything. I put my feelings on hold and I start making phone calls. Martha, whose husband died in October of Parkinson's disease, needed to place him in a facility last summer after he was released from the hospital. She shares with me the types of care she researched in our neighborhood and the one she finally chose. Her husband Arthur was in a Board and Care home, a small facility with six or eight patients that is run by a couple; then she moved him to a hospice facility. Martha was unhappy with the first small facility because she disagreed with the highly opinionated man who ran it. She was forced to change facilities, which was disruptive to her husband and to her. She also informs me of a community in Mesa which has independent living units, assisted care suites and a memory care unit.

Linda and I go to visit this facility, called Legacy House. We are impressed by the site, the layout, the lobby furnishings which look like a hotel and the dining room which resembles a hotel restaurant. The home is quiet; the residents are all well dressed and walking around, some with the aid of walkers. However, the room that Bob would occupy is in the memory care unit, upstairs. The food is the same, but it is served in the locked unit. The day room includes a dining area, an outside patio and a television viewing section, connected to a hallway where there are twelve individual rooms with baths for sleeping. The residents look much older than my husband, mostly feeble-looking women. I feel so sad in this unit. It reminds me of my mother's last months before she died. Both Linda and I feel that Bob would not be comfortable here.

Although we schedule an appointment with the director, we are given the tour by the sales agent, Leslie. After the tour, we sit in her well-appointed office as she asks us to define our needs. We share what we feel Bob needs, a place where there are several men in residence, an open unit with some memory impaired residents and some assisted living residents, outside areas to enjoy the weather, preferably a home which is close by so we would visit him frequently. Leslie phones several nearby facilities for us, asking if they have availability. The place she finds for us is called Mesa House. We drive there next.

Mesa House is a 50 bed facility owned by Senior Living, a corporation that has 557 comparable residential facilities nationwide, five here in the Mesa-Tempe, Arizona area. It is unique in that its assisted living and memory care programs are combined. The external doors are secured so it meets the requirements for memory care. Some residents do not have memory problems so there is a possibility that Bob could befriend someone whom he could see as a peer. There are several men in residence.

The physical plant is lovely, spread out on one floor; the residents can wander freely from their apartments to the activity center, the dining room, the library areas, the television viewing areas, as well as outdoors to the grass-covered area with gliders in the sun and shaded areas. There is a glassed-in porch for times when it is too hot to wander outdoors. There is a beauty parlor where a barber arrives each Wednesday. The décor is vaguely European with Queen Anne styled wing chairs, benches and upholstered couches placed throughout.

The restaurant area has armchairs with upholstered backs and seats, covered with cloth tablecloths protected by a slab of glass. The various sized tables are set with cloth napkins and stemmed water goblets. We are introduced to the resident chef, "Chip" who dresses in black with a black toque worn rakishly to one side, like a beret. He and two helpers cook all the meals on site and they are willing to prepare an alternate dish if a resident requests one. At the moment there are 38 residents living here. The setting fits with Bob's definition of "luxurious." I know Bob won't want to live here. I am afraid he will be angry with me for placing him in any facility. I put these feeling aside, too. I have a job to do.

Next I want to find out how to pay for this level of care. I make an appointment with an attorney who specializes in elder care law. He reviews my husband's military service and shares the four criteria for assistance from the Veteran's Association: service during wartime, honorable discharge from the military, financial assets and monthly income. We qualify on the first two and the lawyer tells me to return in a few years when my husband's assets are reduced. We discuss Arizona Long Term Care plans which are reserved for people with lower pensions than Bob receives. I discover that there is no separation of assets in Arizona; once Bob runs out of money, I will be responsible. This is good to know. It will keep me prudent.

I check with Darcy, Arbor Rose's director, who informs me they have no vacancies at the moment for a resident to enter their home, which is less expensive than Mesa House. It might be possible in the future to move Bob across the street from one facility to the other. Meanwhile, I decide to place Bob at Mesa House. I meet again with the sales agent, Renee, who tells me that we will rent an empty room which we have to furnish. The room rate, on a monthly, no-lease basis will increase yearly. To the room rate is added a service rate which includes whatever services my husband requires. A nurse from Senior Living will assess my husband at the hospital on Thursday and Bob will move to Mesa House on Friday. An appropriate service fee will be established depending on Bob's level of ability with skills of daily living. I am given the fee schedule. This service rate will be adjusted once after 30 days and then again at three month intervals.

No one in the hospital will explain to Bob what will happen. I am told not to escort Bob from the hospital to Mesa House because he will not understand and anyway, he will forget whatever is explained to him. This way it is the hospital and the physicians who are moving him, not me. They are hoping to restore a good relationship between my husband and me; I am afraid they will not succeed.

I make this decision because my goal is to have Bob live close by, so that not only I, but the members of my family also will have an easy drive, so that they will visit Bob frequently. Linda and I begin to shop. As I meet again with Renee, the sales agent for Mesa House, she informs me that some of the residents travel with an aide by van each week to Walgreen's to purchase sundries and to the Village Inn on Thursdays for pie and coffee. She asks my permission for Bob to join this group. I decide to wait and see how Bob adjusts. Then she tells me I am responsible for checking Bob's toilet paper supply and for refilling his bathroom with toilet paper. This is the most absurd requirement I can imagine. During the transition, when Bob will surely think this move is temporary, my bringing in toilet paper will prove to him this is permanent. Bob could not understand last week, when Steve and I brought him new sneakers in the hospital, why we weren't taking him and the sneakers home. My ties to my husband are now to be linked to his consumption of toilet paper? I cannot accept this. I am so upset. Steve volunteers to be responsible for checking the supply. I buy the largest package of toilet paper rolls in the Costco warehouse store, storing it in the garage.

I notice that the bathroom in Bob's unit has no storage for an extra roll, so I purchase two cabinets at Target, which are sold flattened and boxed. Ted volunteers to assemble them and sits on my living room floor to do so. Now Bob will have a place to put his toothbrush and shaving supplies as well as extra rolls of toilet paper. Bob likes to have his belongings in plain view since he forgets about them when they are hidden in a drawer or in a closed cabinet. I want this studio apartment to feel comfortable to Bob, like a home, not like a hospital room.

All of a sudden, it is Friday. I have been so busy I haven't had time to think. I am anxious and concerned that everything goes smoothly with the move. The furniture will be delivered, we will bring the bedding and clothing and set up the room by 12:30 p.m.; the van will drive Bob from the hospital to Mesa House without us being present at all. We are asked not to visit for a few days as he transitions in.

It's morning. Will Bob travel willingly from the hospital without me? Will he understand where he is going? Although I don't want him to blame me for not bringing him home, I want him to miss me. I know that is not logical thinking. I am still looking for him to be who he was, not who he has become.

Grant, Linda's son, wakes up sick and Linda has to take him to the doctor. Renee, the sales agent, volunteers to help me set up Bob's studio apartment, so does Ted. The furniture delivery is delayed, but eventually Linda returns from the doctor's office, Steve babysits for Grant, and Ted, Linda and I drive her SUV and my car, laden with belongings, to Mesa House. We three get the room set up before the van departs to get Bob. I would have been a little less anxious earlier if I realized that the van can't leave to get Bob until I sign the forms releasing him from the hospital.

Everything is accomplished with the amazing help of my children. There is no way I could do this move alone. My children are supporting *me*. I am proud of them and of myself because I asked them a few months ago to check in on me. I have been feeling so tired, stressed and vulnerable that I could no longer have my children seeing me only as the totally independent helper I have always been. I am so grateful that I can count on them; all six of them, Steve, Linda, Ted, Linda's husband Dave, Austin and Grant, too, to be here for me when I need them. I know why we moved to Arizona. In New York, Bob and I were alone, among nine million people.

Meanwhile on the inside, I am a mess. I have acted for all to see, as usual. I don't initially react emotionally to any crisis; I ask questions, I get defensive or argumentative perhaps, but then I make a decision and I act. That's the way it was with the doctor's decision. I heard what he said; I discussed it with my son Ted who had predicted this outcome. I saw the decision to place Bob in a protected environment as a challenge; I made a plan to educate myself about residential facilities and to choose the one that would suit us all best; then I carried out the plan. And I fell apart afterwards, in private, where no one could see.

It is now Friday afternoon and I am home alone. The house is quiet and lonely; I am surrounded by all of Bob's things, our memories, our shared hopes and dreams. I feel so sad and empty. When Bob was in the hospital, I thought it might be fine to have ten days without him at home. But once again I had no respite. During these past five days, I have been so busy; I put all my thoughts and feelings aside. Now, I make myself realize that this move to an assisted living home is long-lasting. It is such a change. I feel so different, so unsettled, so frightened. I have trouble concentrating; I cannot read or write. I don't phone my friends or attend a caregiver's group. I do not watch TV generally, but now I watch reruns of NCIS, a series of crimes solved each week in an hour, and I fall asleep in Bob's favorite chair. I'm awake at 3 a.m. and again at 5, believing I've heard Bob moving about the house. His side of the bed is, of course, smooth and his pillows are plumped.

I wake up again at 8 a.m. on Saturday, phone the staff at Mesa House and I am told not to visit today or on Sunday, to wait until Tuesday. I am distraught. They tell me that Bob is packing and repacking his belongings each time the staff unpacks them and places them in his drawers and closet. He is leaving the table during meal times after each course and needs to be directed back. He doesn't understand where he is, or that he is to remain there.

I feel so sorry for him and for me. I tried so hard to maintain him at home, not anticipating this turn of his illness. Well, I didn't think it would get to this. Others knew, others who have known demented people who have become violent, dissatisfied with life, who lash out at their loved ones. My sister Rita reports that her friend Howie had to remove his wife Carol, who has Early Onset Alzheimer's disease, from one memory care facility and then to place her in another because she was physically abusing the staff. Why will the next one be different? Do they have more staff? I don't know.

273

I share with Bob's children what has transpired; they are not happy, how could they be? We are far away from them in Arizona. They haven't seen their father often during these past five years, so they have not seen the slow progression of his disease. All they have heard is their father's ranting about wanting a divorce or wanting to be in New York. Then they heard but did not see that their father became aggressive and even violent. They would prefer to have their father in a facility which is closer to them. Adam lives in New Jersey; his sisters live in Virginia. There would be no place that would be convenient for all of us. I don't, however, expect the kind of vituperative response I receive. Bob's son Adam writes that although he believes what I have told him is true, he thinks that I am the cause of all his father's problems. *How powerful he imagines me to be. If I could give a person Alzheimer's disease, could I also relieve him of that ailment??* One of his daughters, Lauren, writes in an email that she wishes I get Alzheimer's disease soon, too. I hear no response from the oldest daughter. I guess no news is good news in this case. I am sad for them and for me that there will be no family support for any of us, as we each face the effects of this devastating illness on someone we love, alone.

44 – Initial Visits

Arizona, March 15, 2011

Finally, Steve and I visit Bob on Tuesday afternoon. We approach the long, light stone-sided building with its peaked pink tiled roof, and we see the attached smaller cottage to the left behind a circular drive with a large tree in its center surrounded by grass. We can see Bob's apartment window in the cottage from here, but we must enter through the front door. We stand in the covered portico, ring the bell and are invited in by a young woman wearing a green shirt with a name tag, "Jessica." She smiles brightly as she shows us the sign-in sheet, which Steve fills out for us and Steve sees for the first time, the lovely living room with its gas fireplace, bookshelves, couches, end tables with lamps and cozy-looking reading areas.

We follow the winding corridor toward Bob's room until we see him walking toward us, arms outstretched. "How did you find me here?" Bob asks, holding first Steve, then me in a big hug. "I am so happy to see you. I'm hungry. Do you want to go get something to eat?"

"Sure, but first we brought you some fruit," I answer him. "Let's go put the fruit in your room first."

"I know where it is," Bob says proudly, as he takes a key on a blue wrist band from his pocket. "Number 1-3-9," he continues as he walks confidently down the corridor. He arrives at his apartment and proudly shows us his name printed on an empty memory frame outside his door. "See what it says, that's me," he says. *I feel so sad; he is so child-like now*. Yet Bob has led us to his room. This is a secure place for him. He knows where to find what he needs by himself. He hasn't felt this secure in a long time.

"Let's go to the restaurant and get some coffee," Bob insists. We take the long way around, showing Steve the activity center, the library, more television seating areas. Indeed, one of the staff members invites us into the dining room for coffee and dessert. We meet Chip, the chef, who, Bob says, is a good cook. After snack we walk outdoors and sit in the glider together, holding hands, while Bob is amazed that I found him. We return to Bob's room which looks like a college dormitory room, messed up. Nothing is put into the drawers; most of his belongings are stuffed into the plastic bins I have brought to store extra sheets and towels. I straighten up the room as we show Bob the bananas, grapes and chocolate bars we have brought. Folks are gathering in the living room; it must be time for dinner soon and we depart.

I receive a telephone call from Mesa House asking me to remove his empty backpack, duffel bag and the plastic bins on our next visit, to help Bob stop packing his belongings, which we do on a subsequent visit. On another visit, we observe that now all of Bob's belongings are packed into the plastic trash can liners I was asked to provide. I ask Steve and Bob to go sit outside as I unpack the bags and restock the dresser, closet and bathroom storage spaces. I find many table knives and cloth napkins among Bob's possessions, which he has "shopped" from the dining room.

Austin accompanies us on one visit, but I think Bob confuses him with Ted, as Austin is so grown-up-looking now that he is a college boy. At the next two visits, Bob asks for Steve's brother, Ted, but not by name. "Where's his brother? I want him to come here," he says. "I want to talk to him."

When I arrive alone for visits, Bob complains, "You made the worst decision of your life placing me here," he says, sounding rational and sane and of course making me feel guilty. "I'd rather be in the apartment in New York, where I know where everything is and I can go by myself wherever I want to go." He then shares with me that he is afraid to shave himself with his Bic razors and shaving cream. Steve volunteers to shave him and Steve and I purchase a wet-dry electric razor and return with it.

Bob waves me away from his room, as he removes his shirt for Steve to begin the shaving process. Meanwhile, Betty, the care manager, arrives to check on his window blind, which Bob has told me he removed, but it was only tangled and Steve has already righted it. Betty knocks on Bob's closed door. "Just a minute," Bob says. Then he opens the door.

"May I come in?" Betty asks.

"What are you going to charge me?" asks Bob.

"No charge, Bob," answers Betty. Bob turns to Steve who is waiting in the bathroom for his customer to return. "She wants to come in here and she won't charge us anything," he preens.

"What do you think I'm selling?" asks Betty, and then, thinking better of her response, she backs out of the room, closing the door.

As we walk through the building after the shave, other staff members stop Bob and compliment him on his cleanly shaved face. He says the razor burned him on his neck. Everyone agrees he had several days of growth and it will feel better the next time. Tuesday we return with more fruit and Electric Shave, a pre-shave balm, as well as new aftershave lotion. We feel prepared for a pleasant visit. When half of the shave is completed, Bob says, "Stop. I know what you're doing and it's not going to work."

"What am I doing?" Steve asks. "I'm giving you a shave. It's working better today."

"You're trying to be my friend and it's not going to work." Steve puts the razor down.

Bob walks around all day with half of his face shaved.

Yesterday, I brought Grant with me after school to visit Grandpa Bob for the first time in his new home. We stopped at Cold Stone Creamery for ice cream first and Grant handed Grandpa a cup of ice cream with a spoon and a napkin. Bob said he'd like coffee, so we sat in the dining room while he had his coffee and they both ate their ice cream. Grandpa reminded Grant often not to spill his ice cream. Grandpa showed Grant the pool table and the place where "they play games here." A staff member offered Grant a job for the summer. He could call out the numbers for Bingo. Grant said he could do that. After a 40 minute visit, we left, as Grant had had enough. As I'm driving home, the cell phone rings. It's a worker at Mesa House.

"Dr. Palm," she began, "Your husband has asked me to shave off his beard and moustache. I don't want to do it without your permission," she continued. "He came in to my office just after you left. He said Steve hurt him with the razor and he wanted me to shave him and get rid of the beard and moustache for good. Should I?"

"You have my permission. I only hope he recognizes himself without it, and that he remembers that he asked you to shave them off," I answer. I'm kind of afraid to go there today. I have never seen Bob without his beard and moustache which he has had for half of his life.

I am still responsible for all decisions about my husband's life, large and small. I visit often to observe both his behavior and his relationships with the staff. Sometimes the visits are pleasant and Bob is happy for a snack, a hug or a back rub; other days my visit reminds him of what he has lost and makes him sad or angry. I never know what to expect, so I am anxious before each visit. I leave drained, emotionally spent and sad that Bob is so unhappy. The staff, however, is pleased with his adjustment and do not raise the service fee after the first 30 days.

45 – Insight Redux

Arizona, April 11, 2011

After paying the bill for the furniture for Bob's room and submitting checks for the deposit and the one month advance fees to Mesa House, I receive an invoice in the mail for several thousand dollars, which the corporate office of Senior Living will automatically deduct from my bank account in ten days' time. They have not deducted what I have already paid from their bill. These are the errors and problems I expect to encounter, as a caregiver who doesn't live with the person she/he cares for. I realize I am now just like the women who attended the conference last April in New York at the Academy of Medicine.

I was so unhappy that April day last year, when I discovered that the women who were sharing their stories about care-giving, were all daughters of people suffering from Alzheimer's disease or other dementias, not spouses. It was just one year ago that I discovered how angry I was, living the life of a full time caregiver. I understood then that these women were voicing legitimate concerns about family members they loved, but that they hired caregivers to work for them, to provide the daily supervision and companionship to their loved ones. The focus of the sponsoring agency was to help the audience access the services they need to provide the best care possible for their family members, including when to make the decision to place their loved ones in a residential setting. I have just made that decision.

Every week I speak with the physician's assistant, who is a nurse practitioner. She visits at Mesa House every Tuesday, and will add Bob to her list any time I phone and ask her to see him, or if the staff asks her to add him to her roster. During the first three weeks, she increases Bob's Risperdal medication from 0.25 mg morning and evening to 0.50 mg in the evening and 0.25 mg in the morning because Bob remains agitated. He still packs and unpacks his belongings. He is often angry and he is having a hard time getting settled into the routine. The activities director reports that Bob cannot concentrate on any project and will not sit with others for more than five minutes. Joyce, the nurse practitioner, also increases Bob's Depakote Sprinkles from twice daily to three times daily with an extra dose labeled *prn*, which means 'as needed'.

I vary my visits to see Bob by the day and time of day, because I want to monitor my husband's behavior and to oversee the different staff members. On two different visits, I find pills in his room which he has not taken as directed. Did he spit them out? Did the staff member not wait until she checked that the pills were ingested? I remain with my husband longer on visits when Bob is happy to see me, shortening the length of the visit if he is in a bad mood. Steve accompanies me often, as conversation is easier with three than just with Bob. In other words, I am still completely responsible for my husband's wellbeing, *but I now get to go home.*

Since I have been a full time caregiver for so many years, this new status is a genuine relief. It is now four weeks since Bob moved to Mesa House. I am sleeping better, I have returned to the gym, to my writing. I am still devastated when Bob is verbally abusive. He asked for me one day and complained when Renee told him I was there the day before and will return later that day, "That bitch never comes to see me. When she does come, I am going to hit her with a baseball bat."

On several visits, Bob questions me about his relatives who are no longer alive. He wonders where his cousin Maurice is, and his parents. He asks about his Uncle Louie who died when Bob was a young adult. Bob says he is going to die soon too. I ask him how he is feeling and he says he's fine. I remind him that people who feel fine don't die. I am so sad for him, and I don't know how to respond to his queries. Sometimes I wait, not answering, until Bob says, "Let's change the subject and not talk about sad things anymore."

So do I continue to attend caregiver support groups? I feel guilty, as some of these people keep their spouses at home. Alex and his mother Louise have not attended the group meetings since the winter. Their father/husband has the same kind of aggressive disease progression as Bob. Last I heard he was living at home and attending day care during the week. Perhaps he is in a placement now and that is why they dropped out of the group. Some of the other spouses spend every afternoon at the care home with their loved ones. Ann sits all day with her mother. I don't want to be guilted into doing the same. So I stay away from the caregiver's groups for a while. But by the Friday that marks the third week of Bob's residence at Mesa House, Steve and I have such an emotionally upsetting experience during a visit that we go from the visit directly to the support group meeting. Here's what happened.

Steve and I enter and sign in, a little past one in the afternoon. We are told by the staff member who greets us that Bob is in his room; we see him opening the door to leave his apartment as we walk up the hall.

"What are you doing here?" he yells when he sees us. "Why are you here?"

I answer him calmly. "We're here to visit with you, to sit outside and watch the birds. We brought you some fruit."

"And anyway, what are YOU doing here?" he yells at Steve. "A wife is a wife and a son is a son, and you're not even my son, so get out of here."

"Do you want us to leave?" I ask incredulously.

"Yes," he responds, "and don't come back unless I know in advance that you are coming."

So, shaken, we place the fruit in his refrigerator and leave. We sit in the car, bewildered, then realizing it's Friday, we drive to the Alzheimer's Association caregiver group where we feel welcome. Others share their stories and we sit quietly relaxing; they listen to our event and sympathize, reassuring us that this behavior is to be expected and reminding us not to take this outburst seriously or personally, as Bob's attitude will change by the next visit and he won't even remember this outburst. The group understands that Bob needs to be in a safe, secure environment and they are relieved that I am now safe, too. Mary admits and others agree that they were worried for my safety when Bob was at home. They also advise us to delay the following visit by a whole week, informing the staff what we were doing and why.

Sue, a caregiver from the Arbor Rose support group, telephones me to say that she missed me at the last meeting, and to ask if I am okay. I invite her for lunch before the next Arbor Rose caregiver's group meeting. She arrives without her husband and we have so much to say to each other, we barely eat the salad I have prepared. Sue is considering how long her 24/7 care-giving will continue, until she can place her spouse in a residential setting. Her insurance policy provides for three years of long term care. She wonders how she will decide when to start that process. What happens if he lives longer than the insurance policy's limit? Her husband is compliant, but completely dependent on her. She has to brush and floss his teeth for him.

After lunch, Sue and I arrive at the center for the support group meeting; we are introduced to a woman, Betsy, who placed her husband at the Arbor Rose residential facility just three weeks ago. She shares her concerns about visiting her husband, who fell since he moved to the facility; she had to accompany him to the doctor's office for an x-ray. After the fall and the visit to the doctor's office, Betsy was told not to visit for a week.

"I don't know what to do," she wonders aloud. "Will I be confined to Arizona during the hot summer months or will I be able to visit my family as we usually do together?" No one knows the answer. "Whenever something happens to him, do I have to be in charge? How can I leave?" What if he falls again and she isn't available? I have already made my decision about leaving, and Mesa House will not require me to be present if Bob has a situation which requires a trip for an x-ray, but I understand her anxiety and I am grateful that she is attending this group and voicing concerns which are similar to mine.

So now I understand. I still need support; groups are available. The members are friendly, they are accepting. It is a sign of strength, not of weakness to attend support group meetings. There is no reason for me to feel guilty for placing my husband in a residential facility or for needing help in supporting him during his placement.

So we have come full circle. When Bob and I met twenty-two years ago, he treated me better than I have ever been treated in my life. He catered to me in every way and delighted in doing so. He bought me jewelry; he cooked delicious gourmet meals for me and planned wonderful vacation trips. I was free to establish my private practice and Bob helped with the paperwork. We established new friendships, we entertained and we thoroughly enjoyed our life together. We were a well balanced team. When Bob chose to sell our big house in New Jersey, to reduce the burden he was feeling about the house's upkeep, I went along with the idea, but I really did not want our life to change.

Unfortunately, a year later Bob was able to do less and less. I felt happy to participate in caring for him, as he had always done so much for me, but Bob always resisted being cared for. He enjoyed feeling loved and caressed, but he was never a slippers and a pipe kind of relaxing guy. He wanted to plan and to do, much like me. As he felt less able, he stopped doing. He stopped driving, he stopped sewing; he stopped planning trips. Eventually he stopped managing our money and he stopped cooking. Bob became depressed, as he began to feel useless. His response is not what I would have expected. This disease has robbed him of coping skills as well as judgment, memory and his pleasant personality.

Bob began to need me to be his caregiver five years ago. We traveled from living in a large home in New Jersey to living part-time in two states, New Jersey and New York. We sold our New Jersey house, moving full-time to our one-bedroom apartment. When the neurologist felt Bob needed a hobby room, we moved to a two-bedroom apartment. When that solution didn't work any longer, because Bob had completed the book sorting and the renovations he needed to make to the apartment and he was no longer able to use his sewing machine, I hired helpers to accompany him on trips around the city. Since he refused the help of caregivers who were paid, we built a handicap-accessible house in Mesa, Arizona so my children could assist me in caregiving. We were able to maintain Bob at home for two more years, half of each year in New York and half in Arizona. What began as a labor of love, caring for him became a nightmare for me, as my husband's disease progressed in unexpected ways. As he continued to lose memory function, he began to have paranoid and delusional thoughts which upset both of us. We found a physician who set us on another path, diagnosing Parkinson's disease and providing prescription medications that reduced Bob's paranoid thinking. None of the steps we took helped Bob remain calm for a long period of time. Bob became increasingly aggressive and even violent.

From being the adored, pampered wife, I became the "boss". The balance of power in our relationship shifted. We were able to function with the help of my family and friends. But then I became the enemy. My sweet, devoted husband thought I was poisoning his food; he not only voiced his concerns loudly, he acted on them. When he lashed out at me physically, threatening me with a knife, he needed to be hospitalized. The doctors had no more medicine that would keep Bob calm enough to remain at home.

What I have most dreaded has come to pass. None of us caregivers wants to place our loved ones in a nursing home. Aside from the stories of poor care and disrespect some homes provide, it feels like such a personal loss, like the death of the marriage, which it is. It is also very expensive and threatens to reduce the remaining spouse's standard of living as we age. The decision that others debate and worry about has now been made for me because of the aggressive nature of Bob's disease progression. I am now convinced that my husband needs to be in an environment where he will continue to be safe and secure, where his needs are met by trained personnel, his medications adjusted according to his disease progression, not on the basis of his violent acting-out behavior. Bob will live out his days in Arizona. I will travel for short visits to New York. The children and grandchildren will visit him with me. Our life as we knew it is over.

I didn't know when I began writing this book, how and where it would end. It has only been on rereading that I see that placing Bob in an assisted living facility is the end of my complete devotion of time and effort, providing care for my husband, and thus the logical place to stop. I have shown how early intervention and persistence aided us in having a better quality of life for several years after Bob's diagnosis of "some sort of dementia." I have provided a glimpse into the maze of the health care system as it is today, through different opinions, diagnoses and medications.

I have shared our journey, the difficulties and joys of our families and friends, the way that others came through for us when I was able to ask for help. I have shared the stories of other spousal caregivers I met along the route and how important the stories of their lives were and still are to me. It is funny to me that I saw in Leon's story that my life was easier than his. His wife wanders, has bathroom issues and is afraid of mirrors. Yet, after dining with us in an Applebee's restaurant one evening this winter, Leon turned to me and said that he was more appreciative of his situation, which was so preferable to him than mine.

I introduced you to caregiver classes and support groups, both in person and online, which help me survive the onslaught of this illness, which continues on its path of devastation and destruction. I showed you a day care center for seniors who need supervision and a hospital also limited to the care of a small number of seniors who need psychiatric care. The devotion and the care that is shown by the staffs of these facilities amaze me.

But most of all, I share my experience of these past five years. There is a balance in all relationships, friendly or hostile, that keeps people together. Generally, we went about our lives paying close attention to how we related to each other. We were a well-matched set; a good fit. We knew we had a special relationship and we were grateful for our good fortune every day. When Alzheimer's disease began, the balance shifted; the relationship deteriorated slowly. The person I thought I knew, inside and out, changed slowly and, as the non-demented person, I didn't know really what is happening or why. Alzheimer's disease is not merely the loss of memory. I observed as two independent members of a loving couple, a well-balanced retired team, each with interests of his/her own and a shared life between them, changed slowly into a dependent relationship in which I have to make all the decisions and manage our lives because of the mental deterioration due to Alzheimer's disease. Bob did not like this change any more than I did.

No one talks about Alzheimer's disease except for its memory loss functions. As I have shown, Alzheimer's disease destroys more than memories of person, place and thing. The partner is first pulled into denial along with the person whose memory is failing. When Bob wanted to sell our house I convinced myself that we no longer needed a big house. When he asked for my help selling the house, I jumped on the bandwagon of a more active life in the city. I thought Bob would miss the memories he had of raising his children in the house or of his first wife, who died there. When he at first reduced his activities in the city, I thought he was depressed about losing the house. I nagged, pleaded, cajoled and recommended supplements and psychotherapy. I was showing my frustration and anger at this change in our lives.

It wasn't until Bob began to wait for me in my office all day long that I realized something was truly wrong and we needed medical intervention. I started then to change my life in order to make his more comfortable. When the neurologist suggested that we had made a mistake selling the house, and when Adam, Bob's son, suggested that his father be placed in an assisted care facility a year later, I felt more determined than ever to devote myself to making Bob's life as full of purpose and dignity as I could for as long as possible. I had a goal which sustained me, although I gave up so much of my own life. I gave up my psychology practice, which I had strived for many years to build. I stopped attending cultural, political and entertainment events in the city. Finally, I gave up living in New York, a lifetime goal I had achieved only after marrying Bob.

After reconciling myself to my new role as caregiver, I was no longer angry. We busied ourselves as Bob still does today, packing and repacking belongings. We moved from one state to another, we traveled; Bob repacked and donated books, built bookcases. Bob felt angry, which made me redouble my efforts to please him until finally nothing I could do pleased him any longer, except for my sexual availability. One psychiatrist I spoke with about this subject concluded, "Sex dies with the person." Then I became angry again, realized that I was a prisoner of Alzheimer's disease and set about hiring helpers to assist me in managing my husband's needs for activity and diversion; I felt so stressed and I was always tired.

If you are a caregiver, you know that this book is about one specific Alzheimer-diseased spouse, mine, and that each person with this disease experiences it differently. Each of us caregivers experiences our role differently as well, and I hope you can empathize with me and with my travels and perhaps accept yourself and take care of yourself a little better having read my story. If you are a member of the health care community, perhaps you see how important it is to treat the whole family of an Alzheimer's-diseased person and just possibly you understand the burden placed on the caregivers to sort through the maze of medications and treatments which as of today work only for limited periods of time. If you are a scientist, I hope you see how we are all counting on you to find a cure for this devastating disease. If you are a member of the baby-boomer generation and are concerned about yourself or your spouse, I hope you understand better the need for early intervention and support from family, friends and support groups.

As I have been relieved of the daily responsibilities of a live-in caregiver, I now have time to devote to advocating for the 5.5 million victims of Alzheimer's disease in the United States today and for the projected 10 million sufferers projected for 2038 when the baby boomer generation will reach 82. I will now try to help the public understand this disease better, to raise funds for more scientific research to find a cure for this emotionally and financially draining disease which decimates family savings and cost the federal government billions of dollars in maintaining citizens in residential care facilities. I will also advocate for respite care for caregivers. Family caregivers become a burden to the health care system also, as the strain and stress of care-giving reduces the health of the caregiver and shortens the caregiver's own life by one year for every year he/she spends being a full time live-in caregiver for a loved one with Alzheimer's disease or another mind-stealing dementia. There is no happy ending to my journey; indeed there is no ending now, merely another change of address.

A Final Word

Arizona, December, 2011

Completing this book means more to me than I could possibly imagine. I feel energized, proud, excited and content. I will now be able to speak with others who are experiencing similar issues to mine; I will be able to raise money to help develop more research and clinical trials to find a cure for Alzheimer's disease. It is a disease that destroys every part of the brain – behavior, personality, cognition, comprehension, physical abilities, mental abilities and memory. It is always fatal. There are no survivors; there is as yet no cure. I have also learned that Alzheimer's disease is not limited to the elderly. It affects men and women, young and old, rich and poor, the well-educated and the ordinary person. It is often misdiagnosed and more often diagnosed without any standardized measurement tool. There are some medications which delay the progress of the disease for a while.

I have also learned that caregivers often don't identify themselves as such. They just keep on doing what they have always done: anticipating the needs and providing for the ones they love. We need to recognize that we must care for and about ourselves, have a realistic outlook and reach out to others for assistance. I learned how to nourish myself by eating better, exercising and taking time out for myself each day. I have joined a group that goes hiking in the desert! I am working on community organizing with interfaith grass-roots congregations. I benefit from speaking with others and learning about resources in the community which I share with members of my Alzheimer Association Support group which meets on alternate Fridays.

I feel proud that I am now one of those resources for those of you who read my book or follow me on my blog doctorphyl-heartofpalm.blogspot.com.

My husband now walks with a shuffle and doesn't have much language or any facial expressions, so I can't really tell if he's happy. However, he is able to travel by car to his favorite restaurant, *The Village Inn,* with my son Steve and his brother Irving who is visiting from Florida. Bob is no longer angry; he accepts assistance with skills of daily living and he greets me with a kiss each time I visit.

About the Author

 Dr. Palm, a full time caregiver for her husband since his diagnosis of Alzheimer's disease in 2006, holds licenses as a psychologist in New York and New Jersey. Her professional experience includes 25 years of private practice serving patients of all ages as well as teaching and supervising in hospital and clinic settings. A first grade teacher in the inner city of Newark, New Jersey and in suburban Florham Park, New Jersey she acquired a Master's degree in Psychology at Montclair State University, eventually participating in a school-based support team in Glen Ridge, New Jersey. After achieving the PhD in Educational Psychology at New York University in 1983 and receiving a post doctoral certificate in child and adolescent psychotherapy from Adelphi University in 1990, Dr. Palm was employed by the Jewish Board of Family and Children's Services in Coney Island, New York as a supervising psychologist, while building her practice in Manhattan. The mother of three, she has two grandsons and is grandmother to her husband's four granddaughters.

Made in the USA
Charleston, SC
16 April 2013